CHARGING
AND
COLLECTING
FEES AND
FINES

A Handbook for
Libraries

MURRAY S. MARTIN and **BETSY PARK**

Neal-Schuman Publishers, Inc.
New York   London

Published by Neal-Schuman Publishers
100 Varick Street
New York, NY 10013

Printed in the United States of America.

Library of Congress Cataloging-in-Publication Data

Martin, Murray S.
    Charging and collecting fees and fines : a handbook for libraries / by Murray S. Martin and Betsy Park.
        p.   cm.
    Includes bibliographical references.
    ISBN 1–55570–318–6
    1. Fee-based library services—United States. 2. Library fines—United States. I. Park, Betsy. II. Title
Z683.2.U6M37   1998
025.1'1—dc21   97–43635
                                                    CIP

Contents

List of Checklists and Worksheets

Preface

Librarians frequently talk about "the free public library" and "free access to information," but these phrases mask important realities. Is any information really free? Is any library service free? Every information resource and library service has a cost, since personnel, resources, and other kinds of support all have to be paid for; the question is, Who should pay the price? For the most part, library income is derived from an outside source—the parent institution, a government body, or a corporation. The library's services are a return on the investment made by the community. Most library services are seen as being "free" to the members of the community. Nevertheless, libraries are now considering which services can be "free" in the traditional sense and which should bear a fee or charge. Our intent in *Charging and Collecting Fees and Fines: A Handbook for Libraries* is not to rehash the fee versus free debate, but to look at the increasing need for fees, fines, and similar charges[1] and to provide some guidelines for their calculation.

Most libraries in the United States have not sought to recover costs from their primary user groups, other than from clearly defined services such as database searches, photocopying, interlibrary loan, or document delivery. In this era of privatization, however, we need to look much more closely at the business of librarianship. One early example is the study of city and country library services carried out by Ellsworth Associates in 1991 for the Monterey County Free Libraries.[2] Its purpose was to develop cost centers, determine service costs, and provide data for cost sharing formulas. There will undoubtedly be many more studies as we seek to define more precisely the role of information in society.

There are certainly instances when it seems logical and proper to charge for a specific service, such as replacing a lost library card, that clearly creates costs the library would not otherwise have incurred. Charging fines for user actions (such as not returning books on time) that reduce the access of other users is also necessary. The library's mandate for fees is less clear, however, when such charges create a distinction between regular and value-added services. Are the free alternatives libraries provide as good as fee-based services? What impact do such decisions have on the right to free access to information? These issues must influence any decision on charging for a service. The effect of fees and charges can be differential, and thus detrimental to the library's mission to provide equal access for all.[3]

While the basic and value-added distinction represents a common approach to user charges, another method is to look at specific segments of the community and determine what services can and should be provided free and what should bear a fee. To some extent, this second approach forms the background of the New Zealand approach (discussed in chapter 1), which recommends that libraries segment their users in order to determine what they actually want and what can be supplied by the library. It is most commonly used in establishing special services for business or government, as when the San Francisco Public Library decided to levy charges for special information services offered to local businesses and departments of the city government through the Library Express service. Academic libraries have also set up fee-based services, for both internal and external users, in order to cover the increased cost of the work involved.[4] The fees are often viewed as supplements to the budget that allow the library to undertake work it could not otherwise afford. If such services are for a select group, rather than the general community, these charges seem justified. It is more difficult, however, to contemplate charging regular users for services like interlibrary loan, document delivery, or file transfer, because the very fact that users require these services suggests that the library has somehow failed to meet its primary users' information needs. Nevertheless, given the mixed nature of the developing information network, we can expect that an increasing number of libraries will pass along more of their costs to their patrons.

The majority of existing library charges are for minor services, such as placing a book on personal reserve, processing overdue materials or maintaining rental collections when patron demand cannot be met within the regular budget. Such fees are by no means universally present, nor do they usually represent a significant proportion of a library's total budget. Their purpose is to regulate services, not to raise money: the motivation is not generating income but ensuring that resources are widely available. Many library users simply overlook their personal responsibilities in seeing that public resources are readily available—they keep library materials past their time of return. Can libraries, through the use of deterrent charges, reduce this problem? The evidence to date is that they succeed only partially, but the situation would be worse if they did not impose such charges.

Reevaluation of the library's economic base—whether taxes, tuition, endowment, or business income—has once more raised the issue of who should pay for what and when. It is no longer a philosophical debate of "fee versus fee"; it is the reality of economic planning in the electronic information age, where libraries have to consider how they can offer new information resources while maintaining their traditional base in the printed word.[5] If their budgets are unable to support both, most libraries will be forced to impose charges for the use of new services, whether they wish to or not. The process is already in full force in many larger academic libraries, where access, often for a fee, has joined ownership as a component of collection management, dramatically changing the distribution of expenditures. This is one of the most important shifts in library budgets since the installation of computerized cataloging systems; moreover, it is irreversible. After subscriptions have been cancelled in favor of electronic databases and document delivery, it is impossible either to reinstate them or avoid the costs associated with maintaining the electronic systems. The resulting budget crunch will almost certainly force libraries to impose charges for nonbasic services, although each will develop its own definition of "nonbasic." This problem will remain central to library financial planning for years to come.

As information (particularly in electronic format) becomes subject to contractual agreements with suppliers rather than the simpler rules governing a purchase, libraries are forced to face these issues directly. Can they continue to respond to information needs without charge to the user even when the library itself must pay for such usage, or must they decide whether some services should be subject to fees? Which uses, if any, can and should be considered free? The decision in each case will depend on the nature of the library and the clientele it serves and derive from complex policy and budget issues. Each library must face these issues on its own—general national guidelines cannot replace responsiveness to local conditions. Nevertheless, there must not be a wide divergence in library responses. Local determination of fees and fines has created a wide range of user charges, few of which have any philosophical rationale. This mélange has the side effect of complicating any individual library's interactions with another, as it must cope with differing charges, and suggests that a common determination of appropriate costs may be desirable. Certainly, costs will differ country by country, region by region, even city by city, but it seems excessive for each library in a single state to have different rules about such apparently similar needs as overdue fines.

Charging and Collecting Fees and Fines: A Handbook for Libraries explores these issues. However, the book's purpose is not to seek answers to philosophical questions but to provide practical guidelines for making decisions upon fees, fines, and other charges. The book first explores the economic basis of library service, then examines various activities where the value of a service and the issue of cost recovery might be considered. The possible charges for circulation, notably borrower fees, overdue fines, reserve charges, and nonmember charges, are listed. Most libraries need to recover the cost of providing photocopy and similar services, and suggestions are made about how to determine these charges. Interlibrary loan and document delivery have been greatly transformed recently, and libraries need to consider whether they should recover some of their costs in providing these services. While reference services might seem at first glance to be outside the charge-back setting, there are many recent services that use databases and distant access that generate costs for the library. Should some or all of these costs be recovered? Paradoxically, while benefitting individual library users, cooperatives often generate costs for the participating libraries. Must the individual user bear some of the financial responsibility?

These and other such issues are outlined, and are accompanied by decision-making figures that can help libraries formulate their policies. The figures are deliberately general so that libraries of all types and sizes can use them as worksheets both to develop policies and set specific fees and charges. Where known cost factors exist, they are given; because each library's situation is different, however, no absolute amounts for fees and fines are suggested. A substantial bibliography is included for more information on specific situations.

NOTES

1. See also Marilyn Killebrew Gell, "User Fees I: The Economic Aspect," *Library Journal* (1 January 1979), 19–23; and "User Fees II: The Library Response," *Library Journal* (15 January 1979), 170–173.
2. Ellsworth Associates, *Study of Cities and County Library Services. Final Report* (Palo Alto, Calif.: Ellsworth Associates, 1991).
3. See D. J. Ernest, "Academic Libraries, Fee-based Information Services, and the Business Community," *RQ* 32 (Spring 1993): 393–402.
4. See Murray S. Martin, "Economic Barriers to Information Access," *Bottom Line* 7, no. 1 (Summer 1993): 3–4; and Kevin McCarthy and others, "Explaining Benefit-based Finance for Local Government Services: Must User Charges Harm the Disadvantaged?" in *Charging for Computer-Based Reference Services*, ed. Peter G. Watson (Chicago: RASD, 1978), 3–16
5. Linda Mielke, "Short-range Planning for Turbulent Times," *American Libraries* 26, no. 9 (Oct. 1995): 905–906.

Chapter I

The Economic Basis of Library Services

The governing assumption behind library budgets in the past (at least in the United States) has been that libraries are a public good, or, in the more narrowly defined areas of academic and special libraries, a specific good ultimately benefitting all members of the community. The concept of a public good has become problematic in recent years. A public good is not diminished by use; in the library setting this definition applies most directly to information that is not exclusive, in the sense that one user does not prevent another from gaining benefit, nor does any one person or entity 'own' it.[1] Clearly, this pertains to the ideas and information contained in the books and other materials held by a library for the use of the community, but it becomes cloudier when it relates to databases and similar kinds of information not directly owned by the library. In these instances, any one transaction is unlikely to be repeated in exactly the same form and carries an identifiable and direct cost. Are such services basic or additional? The answer may vary, depending on the role any given service plays within the library. If there is no alternative, which is increasingly the case, then they would seem to be basic, but they benefit only one user and are not the reusable library materials traditionally bought with community money. Access to a shared library database of member-held materials would be free, being no different from a library's own catalog, but a commercial database or service that charges for its usage could be considered a personal service with a resulting charge. The use of a database may well prove quite costly, involving payment for access time, the cost of power, and, possibly, paper and printing costs, unlike the inexpensive circulation of a book. This differential suggests that libraries look carefully at the specifics of each transaction, and structure responses accordingly.

A single library is common property within its own community, and it would seem inequitable to charge for the individual use of materials bought with common funds. The same argument is difficult to apply to external users, and most libraries will charge fees or recover costs for service to nonlocal users. Sometimes, however, an entity such as a state may provide subsidies for service to nonlocal users or enter into agreements with specific libraries for such services. Ultimately, libraries must be responsive to their supporting communities, without neglecting their role within the extended library community, where shared services are often mutually beneficial, for example, interlibrary loan. Library relationships become more difficult when they involve not neighboring libraries, but libraries located around the world. Are there differences between libraries participating in a consortium or other network and those who simply sign on through the Internet? Who is entitled to what can become a major problem. It is interesting to speculate on what differences there might have been had the growth of libraries coincided with the electronic rather than the print age. What we now see as special services would be seen as commonplace. This perspective illuminates the dilemma faced by modern libraries as they try to adapt to new resources and new ways of finding information.[2]

Generally available services, such as circulation and reference, are usually free to local users; that is, no direct transactional costs are recovered. The increasing cost of providing full service through the incorporation of electronic information sources has forced many libraries to reconsider this approach.[3] Even public and private donors who offer hardware and software to libraries cannot reduce the operational costs of using those donated materials. Here the notion of value-added services comes into play. If there is an alternative, e.g., the user can personally look through indexes and catalogs to find the information, the library is justified in charging for an electronic alternative that involves the use of costly equipment and library staff time. This stand may be called into question if the library has cancelled, or never owned, the print alternative. Some libraries have sought to avoid this issue by using funds received from serials cancellations to pay for borrowing or other alternatives. This approach has been used by George Washington University, the Louisiana State University, and the Massachusetts Institute of Technology and illustrates an increasing, but not yet widespread, trend in library budgeting.

In many instances, most clearly in public libraries, there are legal issues. Statutes may define a library's mission and prescribe what services shall be free. There is little compatibility between the various state laws and regulations, and, in many cases, they are silent on this issue.[4] Nevertheless, the fact that some libraries derive their income from public sources makes them more subject to public scrutiny. The same conditions may apply to publicly supported academic institutions, which derive a major part of their income from taxes that are presumably paid by all members of the community, whether they are part of the university academic population or not. Private libraries, on the other hand, are, by definition, for the use of members, and outsiders must expect to pay for any service. In addition, if a library is a depository for government documents it must make deposited materials accessible to the general public. There may also be other restrictions surrounding such federally funded programs.

The library gathers resources—both personnel and material—to meet a set of goals agreed upon by the community. These goals are defined by policy statements but are given reality by the budget process and the actual expenditures of the library. There are often, however, unstated agreements between the financial authority and the library, for example, free library services to students in return for tuition. The latter has been changed subtly by library or technology fees, similar to the all-too-familiar laboratory fees, that have often been initiated or agreed to by student governments; however, the basic understanding that the library's role is to supply needed information to the students has not changed.

A library also relies heavily on certain assumptions about the public benefit of reading and the belief that sharing resources through the library is a wise way to meet community needs. This latter belief provides the rationale for compliance fees and fines, since these charges are instituted to ensure the general availability of library materials, not to provide income. Equally, it can support library-financed interlibrary loan where there are agreements between libraries not to impose charges upon individual users. The increasing shifts in library funding from public sources, mostly in the form of budget reductions, are calling some of these assumptions into question. It is now necessary to demonstrate even more clearly that the library provides a significant return on investment in it. It is also necessary to consider whether it is possible to make charges for certain services part of the general agreement on library support.

OPERATIONAL FACTORS

As distinct from business and industry, the library is unable to define precisely what goods will be needed or when, nor does it have the ability to define its own market other than in very general terms. This latter situation may be changing as libraries carry out more and more market research, aided by new technologies such as electronic mapping, that can help determine the location of new branches or the best route for van service. Automated circulation systems can also be used to determine borrower preferences, although there is a need to preserve user privacy. Even so, it remains difficult to determine exactly what kinds of information will be needed and whether the library should purchase them or simply use "access" methods to deliver them to the user. Library use is also unpredictable. Actual decisions about use are made one at a time by the users, not by the library. While general patterns will appear over time in relation to the term system or to changes in society or the economy, daily activities will continue to be randomly generated. To meet such randomness, libraries must be prepared at all times for at least a minimum level of use. Controlling the hours of opening or of desk service can help direct traffic but cannot change its nature. Each request for service is unique, whether borrowing a book, asking a reference question, or seeking database or interlibrary loan services. Over time, usage can be quantified and categorized, giving the library an outline on which to base future budgets and workflows, but no plan can predict in detail what will be needed or when it will be requested. This unpredictability has hindered libraries in establishing guidelines for budgets, and there is no indication that the electronic age will make the process any easier.

Three other economic factors come into play in the face of this randomness. First, libraries are both labor-extensive and labor-intensive[5]—a result of the individualized nature of their services. It is extremely cumbersome to derive accurate transactional costs that cover all direct and indirect elements. To a certain extent, this is the goal of program and zero-based budgets, but there are many cross-programmatic costs involved in most library transactions. Most economic analysts advise libraries to be careful in analyzing their labor costs, including overheads. This advice has often been overlooked by libraries when they compare services such as interlibrary loan and document delivery, while some transactions, general circulation and reference for example, have scarcely been studied at all. This leaves a wide gap in the analysis of library costs. A much more careful comparison of interlibrary loan and acquisition/cataloging might well have changed library decisions on ownership and access. Without full information on costs, it is very difficult to establish charges or to make proper choices between methods of delivering services. These issues are basic to *Valuing the Economic Costs and Benefits of Libraries*, a study of costs and benefits done in New Zealand, which rightly assumes that unless we determine the relative efficiency of a decision we may well be wrong most of the time.[6] This reflects the fact that in the past most library statistics have been concerned with inputs rather than outputs, for example the Association of College & Research Libraries and the Association of Research Libraries statistical series. Knowing how many books you have may be important, but it is much more important economically to know whether you are meeting your users' needs. The very title of the New Zealand study emphasizes that we should be concerned not only with cost but also value. Placing value on any transaction may be a complex process, but library financial support ultimately derives from the value users place on the services provided. Value is a user concept, cost is a provider concept, and they do not necessarily coincide. These ideas are percolating into other surroundings. Ongoing studies by Glen E. Holt and his economist associates are looking closely at the direct and indirect economic benefits of investment in public libraries.[7] The same kind of analysis is reported from Ontario, where Rod Sawyer is similarly analyzing the economic and job creation benefits of public libraries.[8] These studies suggest that the library contribution to the local economy has been grossly understudied in the past. Indeed, the whole interaction of private and public investment in information has been largely unexamined.

Second, libraries do not control major sectors of their costs, library materials, bibliographic utility charges, telecommunications, and the like, yet they are not structured to "pass on" any increases in costs. This will certainly change in the near future as libraries grapple with electronic information services. The relationship between each individual transaction and its cost will be clearer in this setting, making it easier to calculate and pass on costs. Many libraries already charge for electronic transactions even though they continue to provide other paper-based services free. In such cases, the distinction is based less on actual costs, since these occur in both situations, than on the ease of calculating the expenses for database searches and similar services. Paradoxically, this discriminates against nontraditional users, while it may place barriers between some users and electronic information.

A third, less studied factor is the wide variation between the costs of specific services. Circulating or reshelving a book is, for example, much less costly than answering a reference question or obtaining an interlibrary loan. The costs of acquisition or cataloging and processing may vary enormously, depending on the item involved. Hidden costs, such as those for sending out a bill, a recall notice, or recording a payment, are seldom taken into account even if they are known, and some specific elements of a service, such as replacing paper in copiers or simply keeping terminals clean, have not been analyzed to any significant extent; yet all these are elements in deciding on fees or charges. Although libraries have paid little attention to these kinds of issues they are likely to become much more prominent in the next few years. Libraries have been operating in a comfortable niche between private information services and governmental entities, allowing them to look more carefully at public needs than at costs and accountability. The massive changes in public financing that have characterized the last decade have made such an attitude dangerous. Unless it is possible to demonstrate that the service provided is indeed a public or community good, libraries may well find themselves fighting for any funds at all and, at the same time, having to reconsider the whole range of free services they provide.

Given this background, libraries have been ill-prepared for an economic climate that has emphasized doing more with less and dividing services according to cost and benefit. The result has been severely divergent decisions about what to charge for and what should be free. The process of making these necessary decisions themselves has also become a source of debate.[9] Although placing limits on service is anathema to most librarians, it is still necessary to decide what can best be done within the limits of the budget. It has never been possible for any library to meet all the needs of its users from its own resources. In the future, it may become even less possible. Unless the budget can be expanded to meet not only inflation but the new, added costs[10] some other way of funding information services will have to be found. Some financial authorities think they have found the answer by imposing fees and charges, but as may be found in frequent examples from *LJ Hotline*, the result is not always what was expected, as for instance in an instance where a judge in Pittsburgh threw out a library's case against a borrower because it could not prove that the person had actually been in the library. Charges remain a mere expedient unless they can be worked into the guiding philosophy of the library without causing irreparable damage to the community served.

In terms of charging for such basic services as borrowing books, the answer seems clear. A "book," once purchased, can be used many times for only marginal library expenditure, which implies that any further charges would probably be in the nature of nuisance charges and reduce the library to a kind of rental video store. The cost to the community of not having a library is seldom explored and has not been much exploited by libraries, when, in fact, it is easy to demonstrate that the library acts as a provider to the community in ways that its individual members could never duplicate. This fact is the basis of the library's claim that it is an effective way of distributing to the community as public goods items that would otherwise require massive expenditure by individuals and would also disenfranchise the poor.[11] The advent of newer, mostly electronic information services with a much higher unit cost has made this a difficult stance to maintain in times when "public" money has itself become a scarce commodity, and libraries have difficulties finding funds to purchase the desired range of materials, while also having to cut back on hours or eliminate specific services.

How libraries can recover the extra costs involved is still moot, but eventually the consumer will have to pay, whether individually or collectively. In the first instance the user will pay, in the second, the library. This and similar issues have been under study by the Fee-Based Services Committee of the Public Policy for Public Libraries Section of the Public Library Association for some time. There is a clear division of opinion over what, if any, fees and charges should be levied, while more and more libraries are finding it necessary to recover at least out-of-pocket costs. The report of the committee, *Fees for Public Libraries: An Issue Statement*, sets out general values, principles, and guidelines, rather than establishing exact rules.[12] Nevertheless, it emphasizes that fees should be charged only for services beyond those considered basic and attempts to provide some guidelines for determining what those services could be. Fines, however, are specifically excluded from consideration as fees. Libraries thus find themselves in the midst of an uncertain battleground, without any clear guiding principles. There are several players—publishers, vendors, libraries, and users—but the roles assigned to each are less than clear. Who should assume the responsibility for providing information to the individual user, and what should be the cost?

CATEGORIES OF FEES AND CHARGES

Fees and charges can be divided into internal—those levied on the library's own community—and external—those levied on outside users, institutional or personal. They can also belong to one of several categories. These are not always mutually exclusive, and the following list provides definitions and examples of fees and charges.

Defining Charges

- **Uniform transaction charges**, 50¢ for a personal reserve; $5.00 for an interlibrary loan, $5.00 for a videotape

- **Compliance charges**, overdue fines or lost book payments

- **Restrictive charges**, $50.00 fee for interlibrary loan to an outside library (to discourage use)

- **Generalized user fees**, membership fee for outside use of a library

- **Fees for specific services**, use of databases

- **Partial cost recovery charges**, out-of-pocket costs for photocopying, processing charges for lost books

- **Total cost recovery charges**, repayment of both direct and indirect costs for database use, interlibrary loan, or for lost or mutilated books

- **Trade-off payments**, balancing charges for outside use within a group of cooperating libraries

---

This short list suggests the wide range of economic decisions a library must make as it considers any application of fees and charges. It is important to remember that the process of recovering a fee, fine, or other charge also has a cost. In fact, the processing cost may well exceed the money recovered, and that should be kept in mind when determining the amount to be charged or whether an alternative system of enforcing compliance may be more effective. For example, a prohibition on further borrowing may be more effective than any fine system.

Beyond these are the considerations that must go into any decision to develop a complete fee-based service to any group, whether internal or external, when both direct and indirect costs need to be recovered. Here the effect on the library's not-for-profit status must also be considered. In fact, many libraries have set up their fee-based services on an independent basis to preserve that status. Document delivery, as distinct from interlibrary loan, falls into this category unless the library has fund reserves that can be used to pick up the cost. Some of these issues were examined by Pederson and Gregory and will be referred to later in the appropriate chapters.[13] Finding the right mix can prove difficult and must be guided by community need. Examples of an alternative approach are the use of funds from cancelled serial subscriptions to support document delivery by the Massachusetts Institute of Technology, the Louisiana State University, and George Washington University. Similar questions need to be answered when considering use of external services such as consultants for specific activities or outside companies for such services as photocopying. The basic issue is which decision advances the local objective of providing the best possible information service for the community involved.

All decisions regarding charges or fees should be made primarily with regard to their compatibility with the library's mission, and only secondarily with their potentiality as income sources. This is not, however, a universal rule. Many special libraries must generate their income by charging for services. An excellent study by Albert J. te Grotenhuis and Selma J. Heijnekamp outlines the cost recovery procedures used in a special library in Holland, and its findings could be true of any special library.[14] A survey of London libraries by Yvette Tilson indicates that charges of one sort or another are widespread and that some libraries are expected to generate a significant proportion of their income from fees, fines, and other charges.[15] Mission and income tend to come together when it becomes a question of whether or not the service in question can be provided within the regular budget. Recovering costs may be the only way the service can be provided, and this needs to be made clear to users who may otherwise overlook such a fee's direct relationship to the service and see it as a way of adding to the library's income, a kind of hidden tax increase.[16] Care also needs to be taken to ensure that the charges do not unduly restrict access to the particular service, particularly by any disadvantaged group of users. It is clear that charging for library services is becoming the norm, even when the library is publicly supported, but it is still important to determine what level of charges is appropriate.

Cost Recovery

- Should the library recover all costs, direct and indirect?

- Should it seek to recover the entire cost of providing a particular service or only the associated direct costs?

- Should it differentiate between regular and special services?

- Should the library or the user assume the costs related to special information needs?

The issues and decisions libraries must consider are seldom clear and involve community, administrative, library, and individual goals, which are not always in agreement. The library's goal is to decide what kinds of services it ought to provide; however, there are not always sufficient support dollars to achieve these ends. There will always be some cases where a combination of public and private (user) funding is necessary, hence the need to determine the kinds of fees and charges that will be levied. Even aggressive solicitation of donations cannot take the place of regular operational funds, though it may make it easier to install expensive equipment or systems and thus reduce their later impact on service costs. Libraries face a future that demands aggressive search for donations, whether from public or private sources, continued demonstration of the need for general funding through peak performance, and decision making about charging for services. While many librarians see fees as inevitable, others view them as intrusive upon the roles and purposes of libraries.[17] Nevertheless, only some combination of donations, funding, and fees will enable libraries to continue functioning as information providers within the new information society.

NOTES

1. See Malcolm Getz, *Public Libraries: An Economic View* (Baltimore: Johns Hopkins University Press, 1980); Selma Mushkin and Richard M. Bird, "Public Prices: An Overview," in *Public Prices for Public Products*, edited by Selma J. Mushkin (Washington, D.C.: Urban Institute, 1972) 3–25; and William J. Baumol and Matityahu Marcus, *The Economics of Academic Libraries* (Washington, D.C.: American Council on Education, 1973).

2. For example, see the article by Karen Commings, "Libraries in the Future—Carroll County Public Library Offers Internet Access," *Computers in Libraries* 14 (April 1995): 14–15.

3. There are many notes, letters, and news items on this point, but it is made with some clarity by David Taylor in "Serials Management: Issues and Recommendations," in *Issues in Library Management: A Reader for the Professional Librarian* (White Plains, N. Y.: Knowledge Industry Publications, 1984), 82–96, where he points out that unlimited free photocopying could easily bankrupt any library and that the same could be true of unlimited access to databases.

4. Pete Giacoma, *The Fee or Free Decision: Legal, Economic, Political, and Ethical Perspectives for Public Libraries* (New York: Neal-Schuman Publishers, Inc. 1989).

5. Douglas M. Knight and E. Shepley Nourse, ed., *Libraries at Large: Tradition, Innovation and the National Interest* (New York, Bowker, 1969).

6. Coopers & Lybrand, *Valuing the Economic Costs and Benefits of Libraries* (Wellington, N. Z: New Zealand Library and Information Association, 1996).

7. Glen E. Holt, Donald Elliott, and Christopher Dussold, "A Framework for Evaluating Public Investment in Urban Libraries," *Bottom Line* 9, no. 4 (1996): 4–13.

8. Rod Sawyer, "The Economic and Job Creation Benefits of Ontario Public Libraries," *Bottom Line* 9, no. 4 (1996): 14–26. This article, and that cited in note seven, has an excellent bibliography.

9. This is made clear in a report by the Urban Library Coun-

cil in 1993, which found that 47 percent of the states had not addressed the issue of fees, while 35 percent prohibited fees on basic services, 14 percent permitted fees on any services, and 6 percent prohibited any fees. (Reported in *Library Journal*, 1 May 1993) A report of the Public Library Association, Public Policy for Public Libraries, Fee-Based Services Committee also indicated that there were greatly divergent views among its members (*Public Libraries* 33, no. 6 [Nov/Dec. 1994]: 333).

10. Murray S. Martin, "Stagnant Budgets and Their Effects on Academic Libraries," *Bottom Line* 3, no. 3 (1989): 10–16; and "The Implications for Acquisitions of Stagnant Budgets," *The Acquisitions Librarian* 2 (1989): 105–117.

11. Laura Kahkonen, "What Is Your Library Worth?" *Bottom Line* 5, no. 1 (1991): 9.

12. Public Library Association. Public Policy for Public Libraries Section. Fee-Based Services Committee, *Fees for Public Libraries: An Issue Statement* (Chicago: PLA, 1996).

13. Wayne Pederson and David Gregory, "Interlibrary Loan and Commercial Document Supply: Finding the Right Fit," *Journal of Academic Librarianship* 20, no. 5/6 (November 1994): 263–272.

14. Albert J. te Grotenhuis, and Selma J. Heijnekamp, "The User Pays: Cost Billing in a Company Library," *Bottom Line* 8, no. 4 (1995): 26–31.

15. Yvette Tilson, "Income Generation and Pricing in Libraries," *Bottom Line* 8, no. 2 (1995): 23–26.

16. Arlene M. Dutchak, "A Look at What's Happening in Alberta: User Fees: Hidden Taxes or Free Enterprise?" *Pacific Northwest Library Association Quarterly* 58 (Spring 1994): 11–12.

17. For example, the issues raised by Wendy Smith, "Fee-based Services: Are They Worth It?" *Library Journal* 188 (15 June 1993): 40–43; and Mary Ann Trail, "Fee-Based Services: Do They Have a Place in Our Libraries?" *New Jersey Libraries* 27 (Winter 1993-94): 22–24.

Chapter 2

User-Related Fees and Charges: Circulation and Similar Services

Libraries commonly use financial incentives to ensure compliance with rules relating to the use of resources.[1] Usually, these are fines for overdue and lost books, but there are several other issues, such as membership fees or charges for specific kinds of use (e.g., reserving a specific book or other item). Such constraints are necessary to ensure that some library users do not intrude on the rights of others, for example, by keeping books out of circulation beyond their allotted time. Some will, however, dispute the right of the library to impose fees and fines when there is no demonstrated need for the return of the materials in question. Others, as a type of a social protest, may deliberately keep materials beyond their return date or arrange for a continuous series of recalls to keep the materials off the shelves. These issues may make the enforcement of any rules and regulations difficult and must be dealt with on a case-by-case basis. The aim of this chapter, however, is to review compliance charges and provide some guidelines for their development or review.

The basic goals of any lending enforcement policies are to enable readers to share the library's resources and ensure such materials' continued ownership by the library. Recall for another user, for example, meets both conditions. Libraries must also provide for the needs of users who need checked-out materials immediately. Few libraries are able to provide sufficient multiple copies of popular books to meet immediate demand, hence the development, in public libraries, of duplicate collections subject to rental charges. In the academic library, books placed on reserve are intended to be equally available to all potential users; however, the institution is seldom able to provide enough copies, nor can it guarantee that they will be available to nonstudent users. In such circumstances, compliance charges are adequately justified.

The ways in which such fees and charges should be calculated have not previously been subject to extensive scrutiny. A study conducted by Burgin and Hansel[2] appears to be the most comprehensive examination of overdue charges to date; the Urban Library Council conducted a survey in 1993 that showed little, if any, uniformity. In fact, overdue and lost book charges appear to be eclectic rather than rational.[3] In addition, Burgin and Hansel's study indicated little, if any, correspondence between library policies and the successful enforcement of rules. It suggests that libraries seek more efficient ways of enforcing policies. There are, however, some potential side-effects of policing circulation. For example, judicial actions have recently taken place over overdue and lost books. While some libraries have been upheld in their search to recover books or levy fines, others have been rebuffed, as in the case of Dormont Library in Pennsylvania, where a judge threw out a claim for $172.58 against a borrower who stated that she may have returned the book to another library.[4] This ruling implies the need for a much higher level of library record keeping and closer scrutiny of cooperative lending and suggests that libraries need to build such considerations into their automated systems. Most problems will never reach the courts, and many libraries have decided to use private firms in recovering overdue materials or the resulting fines. As with legal actions, such recourses may be governed by state legislation. They may also generate an inappropriate level of public attention on the library and are not recommended as standards by which libraries should determine their policies.

Now that computerized circulation systems are becoming more common, it may be more appropriate to impose borrowing restrictions than to attempt to recover fines. Again, statutes may at least define what public libraries can do, and the actions of such bodies as academic senates may determine the alternatives available to academic libraries. Special libraries face entirely different sets of questions, and maintaining collegiality may be more important than imposing fees and charges. It is difficult, for example, to require a partner in a law firm to return books that may be requisitioned for an important legal suit. Nevertheless, in all library settings, the library has to determine how it will ensure compliance with general borrowing regulations and benefit the whole community. The resultant policy decisions leading to the imposition of fees or fines should be incorporated into a publicly available handout, for, unless the information is made available in this manner, there may well be disputes about the library's decisions. In the case of public libraries, any such document should have the approval of the Board of Trustees, while academic libraries may need administrative or academic senate approval.

GENERAL USER FEES

Few libraries, other than private ones, impose a general user or membership fee. Those that do tend to be rental libraries or those that provide distant services to their users, though even these kinds of charges may be less possible in an era when distance learning is becoming more common. Libraries may use such fees to generate revenue for the maintenance of services. They may also seek to establish different levels of users. Some may have full privileges, including borrowing, while others may simply have the right to use the library without being able to borrow materials. Most libraries, on the other hand, have to face the question of how to deal with outside users. In public libraries this may be determined by statute or by state or regional agreements that provide for mutual access. Academic libraries are less likely to encounter this type of situation, but may, instead, be involved in shared access programs, whereby users have access to all cooperating libraries and may sometimes be subject to added charges. This can be resolved by the purchase of user cards (not necessarily personal) or by agreements on what each library should be responsible for in terms of overdues or lost books, as is the case within the Boston Library Consortium. It is more common, however, for academic libraries to ask for some kind of annual membership payment, based on the usage being sought.

Some libraries, seeking to extend their community support, develop Friends Groups. The University of Connecticut, for example, charges a $25 membership fee for community users, but only $20 for Friends, who also pay a group membership fee. Such an approach can also be used to provide corporate service to the business community, issuing a specific number of cards in return for a supporting payment, perhaps in the class of corporate sponsor. Business support is most likely to be pursued by public academic libraries, since they are already dependent on public financing and cannot exclude supporting taxpayers by requiring membership fees, even though the latter may be asked to pay for special services. Private academic libraries may levy charges relating to the cost of providing service to individuals: Yale University, for example, charges $720 per year for full service to an outside borrower. The range of possibilities is endless, but all libraries should think carefully about the effects of their decisions.

Effects of Membership Fees

- Will charging for service to some constitutents affect services to others?

- Can the distinctions be drawn clearly enough to prevent charges of discrimination?

- What is included in each kind of service?

These issues will continue to haunt all public entities. There are no easy answers, because each library operates within a different nexus of local funding, expectations, and directives, as well as within the broader world of libraries and information as a whole.

SPECIFIC USER CHARGES

Library budgets are primarily determined on the basis of the cost of providing services for which their supporting community is willing to pay. Within this limitation, libraries are able to determine whether added charges are permissible. Discussion here will be limited to general use. Such services as interlibrary loan, document

---

Figure 2.1 Checklist for Determining Membership Charges

	Yes	No
Is it legal to charge for membership privileges?	—	—
Do such charges apply only to external users?	—	—
Are there any differential charges?	—	—
Community users	—	—
Friends of the Library	—	—
External users	—	—
What kind of charge is appropriate?		
Full cost recovery?	—	—
A nominal charge only?	—	—
Is there a charge for replacing a library card?	—	—
Is it the full cost?	—	—
Is it a nominal charge?	—	—

---

delivery, photocopying, and database use will be discussed in subsequent chapters.

Library Cards

Few, if any, libraries charge for the first issue of a user card. In fact, public libraries may be specifically prohibited from doing so. Private libraries will, of course, have a membership charge. This can be part of a general membership fee but may be levied separately. Many libraries, however, will charge for the issue of a replacement card. This charge appears to be valid, because the cost of creating a new user card is substantial, involving not only the cost of the card itself and the staff time involved, but also the cost of reconfiguring the borrowing register and providing a new borrower number. $10.00 is suggested as an appropriate charge for card replacement.

Outside Borrowers

A decision must be made on what regulations apply to external borrowers. Should there be equal charges for community and outside borrowers? Does an outside borrower have equal rights with all other borrowers, or are the rights restricted?

Each library must determine what charges must be associated with each kind of service. This was part of the intention of the New Zealand initiative. Is the goal to recover the total costs involved? In this case, the external borrower fee must be derived from the general cost of serving an individual user. Is the cost to be related to the political benefits derived from enrolling another library supporter? In that case, some degree of subsidization may be justified.

Compliance Charges

Any library has an interest in having its holdings available for circulation, and charges for overdue, lost, or damaged materials that insure this require some kind of enforcement mechanism. There is little agreement within the library community over how to calculate and levy such charges. Most libraries calculate overdues based on the number of days, at a given amount per day as low as 5¢. Some libraries remit or reduce overdue charges for specific user groups such as senior citizens, but these are exceptions and do not interfere with the general applicability of the rules. There may be a grace period during which the books can be returned without any fine actually being paid. In many academic libraries, a week is allowed. For example, the University of Connecticut library charges 25¢ a day per item with a maximum of $7.00 but allows an eight-day grace period. On the other hand, if an overdue book is recalled, the charge becomes $1.00 a day, with a maximum of $15.00, and only one grace day is allowed. The grace period can be justified on the grounds that it costs the library a great deal to calculate the fine, accept payment, make change if necessary, and keep records of the amounts received in fines. There are no readily available figures for these costs, but in general financial situations, the cost of generating a bill, tracking payment, and crediting the appropriate account may well cost more than $20. These issues must always be kept in mind when deter-

Figure 2.2 Checklist for Establishing External Borrower Regulations

	Yes	No
Will they be subject to the same rules as other library users?	—	—
Will there be differential rules, for example, fewer items charged out or shorter loan periods?	—	—
Should some differential cost be assigned to corporate or personal users?	—	—
What kinds of services are covered?		
Borrowing?	—	—
Access to electronic databases?	—	—
Are all users subject to the same kinds of charges for photocopy?	—	—
Are all subject to the same kinds of limitations on the numbers of books borrowed, or overdue and recall charges?	—	—

Libraries seeking to extend their user base must address the following questions and consider the attitudes of their supporting community. The answers will determine the charges levied.

	Yes	No
Can the library support the extension of its services to others without substantial charges to outside users?	—	—
Should it seek to recover added costs?	—	—
Should outside users bear only a proportionate share of the total cost?	—	—
Should they be made responsible for all added costs?	—	—
For a share of the general cost of providing library service?	—	—
Is it important to make the library a vital part of a larger community rather than ensure that the library recovers added costs?	—	—

Figure 2.3 Checklist for Setting External User Charges

	Yes	No
What services are covered?		
Borrowing library materials?	—	—
Interlibrary loan?	—	—
Database services?	—	—
Other services?	—	—
What cost recovery basis should be used?		
Out-of-pocket costs only?	—	—
Full cost recovery?	—	—
Should there be differential charges?		
Friend of the Library?	—	—
External library user?	—	—
Consortial member?	—	—
Any other regulations?	—	—

mining overdue charges, since it is not simply a matter of recovering an overdue book but of covering the costs involved.

Most public libraries are permitted to retain the money so received as income, but many academic institutions require that any fine money collected be returned to the central accounting office. It may be not entirely lost, since the library may be asked to calculate the likely revenue from such transactions in advance, and that sum is allowed for in the library budget. The rationale behind this stance is that for the most part, fine money represents staff time that is already part of the budget. The calculation is extremely difficult, given the number of variables involved and can be, at best, only an approximation. If possible, the governing authority should be persuaded that such revenue should accrue to the library, which should, in turn, ensure that the revenue thus gained is used wisely to support library and institutional goals.

USE OF LONGER PERIODS IN CALCULATING OVERDUES

Occasionally, overdue fines have been based on longer periods, say a week, with substantial increases as the period becomes longer.

Figure 2.4 Checklist for Determining Compliance Charges

	Yes	No
Are these charges universal?	—	—
Is there any difference between internal and external users?	—	—
Overdues		
Are charges based on the number of days overdue?	—	—
Are they cumulative?	—	—
Is there any limit to the charges?	—	—
Is there a charge for overdue processing?	—	—
Other Charges		
Is there a time when the item is deemed lost?	—	—
What is this time limit?		
Is there a processing charge for replacement?	—	—
Is this charge remitted if the item is returned?	—	—
Is there a charge for noncompliance with a regulation, e.g., not rewinding a tape or videocassette?	—	—
Is the borrower subject to other controls, e.g., withdrawal of borrower privileges?	—	—

There are no clear indications as to whether this is a more successful approach, but Burgin and Hansel's study seems to indicate these longer periods are better.[5] In fact, some libraries will presume a book lost after one or more months and send a bill for replacement. If the original loan period is substantial, say a term or even a year, as in many academic libraries, overdue procedures should be modified to reflect this difference, because charging for one or two days is nonsensical. The principal goal is not revenue but the return of the loaned item, and all policies should be structured with this in mind. Positive community relations are also a factor: increased revenue is not a suitable substitute for user satisfaction and support. Nevertheless, libraries need to make it clear that compliance with borrowing regulations is basic to being able to support community expectations. Making this connection enables the library to lose its image as a petty scrutineer and show that its concerns are indeed with the needs of the community at large.

ALTERNATIVES

Other methods of enforcement may prove more practical. Libraries with automated circulation systems have found it satisfactory simply to block user privileges for those with a given number of overdue books, not reinstating the borrower until the books are returned or accounted for. The University of Connecticut circulation policies, for example, state explicitly the reasons for the suspension of borrowing privileges, and differentiate between classes of user. This kind of policy statement is essential, and should be readily available to users, because it forms the basis of the agreement between the user and the library. Another method of enforcement available to academic libraries is the prevention of the issue of grades or graduation records to delinquent students. In these cases, the library establishes a routine with the registrar or bursar whereby the names of delinquent students are submitted, together with the amount owed in fines, and completion of the academic process is dependent on return of the books and payment of fines or other charges.

Another method, particularly when there are no limitations on the numbers of books that can be borrowed or are also long-term loan periods, is to incorporate periodic recalls as part of an inventory system. This is possible only with automated circulation systems, may require the printing lists for borrowers with many books, and can be quite costly. The actual existence of the materials out of the library for a long time needs to be ascertained, and hence the link to periodic inventories. This is most likely to apply to academic libraries. Other types of libraries need, however, to realize that their collections are a capital investment that needs to be protected and that recalls of overdue materials are part of that process. Often, users tend to think of borrowed materials as belonging to them rather than to the library; many academics rationalize their extensive office collections of library materials as items no one else would want.

SPECIAL CASES

There are some classes of library materials for which short term, daily, or even hourly overdue charges are justified. A prime example is the reserve reading collection in an academic library, since its usefulness depends upon providing prompt supply of the materials so reserved. There can be different issue periods, varying from an hour to two or three days or even a week. The fine levied should relate to the period of loan. Strict enforcement is essential: these fines are being levied not as a punishment but to protect the rights of other users, who have been deprived of access. The amount charged should be substantial though not punitive, since it is not a matter of possible other use, but of almost certain other need. Besides, the nature of the service will also involve considerable staff time, and continual calculating of cumulative fees is an expensive activity. For books and other materials lent by the hour, the charge could be an initial fee of $2.00 plus 50¢ per hour if overdue by more than an hour. For those lent in periods of days, the basic fine could be $5.00, with a further charge of $1.00 per day.

This reasoning also applies to a public library's rental collection of popular reading, which is intended to enable readers to gain quick access to high-demand materials. If a reader abuses this privilege, it is appropriate to impose a substantial fine. Here the collection has been established to enable users to gain quicker access to wanted materials than if they had to wait for the title to reappear in the general collection. Again, this is outside the regular routine and can be subject to different kinds of fines from regular overdues. In addition, there may be issues regarding the circulation of videos in public libraries, where there is an element of direct competition with other commercial outlets.[6] Fines may be levied if audio cassettes and videos are not rewound. This protects the integrity of the materials and makes them readily useable by the next borrower. Staff time has to be spent to make sure that the next user can, in fact, use the materials. A charge of $5.00 or $10.00 is quite reasonable in these circumstances.

LOSS AND DAMAGE OF LIBRARY MATERIALS

It is inevitable that some library materials will be lost or damaged by users. The library has a legitimate interest in their replacement or repair and should not have to bear the cost of doing so. There are two possible approaches: full cost recovery and partial cost recovery. In most circumstances, full recovery of the loss seems most appropriate, because the library will have to repeat the process of acquisition and cataloging, but it is also possible that the materials may have been in poor condition already, in which case partial recovery may be appropriate. These charges should be added to any fines already incurred for having overdue materials.

Replacement Cost. The first issue is determining the replacement cost. While it may appear easy to consult such tools as *Books in Print* to determine the cost, older, foreign, or rare materials are not listed there. For the most part, recent materials can be assessed at their published price. The library may or may not receive a discounted price from its suppliers, but in the case of replacing a single book or other item, the library may have to go outside its normal buying routines. It will probably have to pay dealer costs or postage, which may raise the price beyond that published. For older materials it may be necessary to go through secondhand or rare book dealers, again raising the internal library costs; there are appropriate information sources for determining such prices (*American Book Prices Annual*). There will, however, always be cases that fall outside these parameters, and the library will have to determine what kinds of charges it will levy. It may not always be easy to determine the cost of replacing a particular book, and libraries may wish to follow some kind of standard charges. In all cases there will be the issue of deciding whether to charge other processing costs.

Standard Charges. Some libraries have simplified their approach by charging standard costs for books (hardcopy or paperback) and other materials such as videos, CDs, and cassettes. In the case of books, that could be $50.00 for hardback books in a college setting, or $25.00 in a public library setting, and $10.00 for a paperback. These prices should be determined from the library's own records and adjusted as prices in the marketplace change. This is one of the most difficult factors to control. Whereas most public bodies will set policies, including charges, for a long period of time before revising them, libraries face a market where prices change rapidly, the cost of finding an out-of-print item varies with the item involved, and the very existence of the item in question may not be certain. These considerations suggest that standard prices may not always be practical, but they may be the simplest way of solving multiple problems without expending too much staff time.

Processing Charges. Replacing an item involves purchasing and processing. While there will be differences in the costs any one library incurs, it is possible to derive a standard processing fee. $15.00 to $25.00 seems reasonable when there are catalog records in existence (if the new copy has different bibliographic requirements costs will rise). There may also be a fee for institutional processing of the calculation and payment of the fine. In many situations this cost is substantial, on the order of $20.00, and would be nonrefundable, even if the item were returned. This is justified by the fact that the library has already incurred at least some of these costs. There are problems associated with this situation, and libraries setting charges will have to rely on precedents from other libraries.

Some patrons may offer to replace the materials themselves. Some libraries have a rule against accepting this kind of offer, but it is hard to go along with that stance, since the borrower has voluntarily spent time and money in doing so. There would still be internal processing costs to take into account, and these should be charged to the user, although they may be less than if the library had had to commence the purchasing process itself.

Damaged Materials. Damaged materials present a different issue. Some may require complete replacement, others may require only mending or rebinding. The costs involved in either process should be recovered. Sometimes the damage will occur within the library. Deliberate mutilation is by no means uncommon, but can seldom be assigned to a specific individual. Here, the costs may be the acquisition of replacement pages or the item's complete replacement. Where direct responsibility can be assigned, the costs incurred should be recovered. Libraries should be aware that such laborsaving devices as bookdrops can cause damage to materials. The University of Connecticut, for example, conducted a campaign to discourage such returns by showing in a display the kinds of damage that can occur.

Many academic institutions do not allow libraries direct recovery of charges made for lost and damaged materials. This is somewhat shortsighted, since the aim is to restore the library's capital investment in the materials in question. It should be possible for the library to assign such charges back to the library materials budget, thus allowing for the purchase of necessary materials. The importance of this differentiation between library materials as capital expenditures and operating costs was underlined by a decision of the Seattle School Board, which denied the school superintendent's appeal for a property tax to buy more books.[7] Libraries should seek, wherever possible, to have the purchase of materials classified as a capital expense.

RECALLS AND SIMILAR PROCEDURES

Library materials are issued with the understanding that, if another user wishes to consult the materials in question, they can be recalled. Recall notices generally specify a date for return, which should allow for the time taken in communication. This procedure might not be invoked if the recalled items are due shortly, but delayed until they become overdue. It can, however, be argued that exceptions make the application of any procedure cumbersome, and, in any case, the notice is simply a warning that the materials are needed back in the library. The costs of sending out a notice, whether by mail, telephone call, or campus delivery service, are real. Failure to comply should be subject to a substantial charge, perhaps $10.00, and the charge should be levied if the materials are not returned by the specific date required.

Computer systems can help by suspending borrowing privileges. Academic libraries sometimes face a serious problem if users, whether faculty or students, are away from the institution or attending a conference. The former is sometimes addressed by re-

---

Figure 2.5 Checklist for Establishing Charges for Lost or Damaged Library Materials

	Yes	No
Lost Materials		
Are costs assigned directly to the borrower?	—	—
Replacement cost?	—	—
Processing costs?	—	—
Administrative costs?	—	—
Are any of these cost remitted if the materials are returned?	—	—
Is the library prepared to accept a replacement?	—	—
Damaged Materials		
Is the charge related to an existing condition?	—	—
Is the charge the direct result of borrower use?	—	—
What kinds of costs are involved?		
Rebinding?	—	—
Replacement of pages?	—	—
Replacement of the whole item?	—	—
How much of the resulting costs should be charged to the user?		
All costs?	—	—
Some costs, e.g., rebinding, costs of photocopying?	—	—
Are there special costs involved?	—	—
Unreplaceable items?	—	—
Costly repairs?	—	—

Figure 2.6 Checklist for Establishing Costs for Recalled Materials

	Yes	No
Is there a charge for the initial request?	—	—
Is there a penalty for noncompliance?	—	—
Is unreturned recalled material treated as lost?	—	—
Are noncompliant borrowers barred from further borrowing?	—	—

quiring that all faculty leaving the institution return all borrowed library books before departure, or at least provide the library with permission to recover them from their offices. Such rules are difficult to enforce. Where books are held in user studies or carrels, most libraries reserve the right to recover them for use by other patrons. Here the issue is resolving mutual user needs rather than library rules, so the decision has to be determined by library policy regarding user rights. The ideal is that all users should have equal access to the library's collections, but clearly, if those collections are being used, some items will always be on loan to individual borrowers. This is a case of the rights of borrowers being in conflict rather than of the comparative rights of the library and the borrower. In some cases, libraries attempt to reconcile these needs by holding collections within the library and not permitting borrowing, as for example, the New Zealand Collection in the Auckland Public Library, but this still gives rise to the problems associated with having materials in current use and providing adequate copying facilities, quite apart from the difficulties associated with the overuse of limited collections. To this may be added the logistics of dealing with author lending rights, if these are in force in the country in question.

PERSONAL RESERVES

Most libraries provide a mechanism whereby users can request materials already on loan to another user. This kind of service is highly desirable, but also involves costs to the library, at least the cost of sending out a notice to the present borrower (recalls) and of sending a notice to the would-be borrower. These costs are often significant and can be considered recoverable. Even public libraries that are prohibited by law from charging per use are usually able to charge for placing a personal reserve. In most cases the charge is minimal, say 50¢, but libraries should consider the real cost, which is more likely to be $2 to $4.00. Policy will determine what charge should be levied, but it seems reasonable to charge the actual cost. Any lesser amount requires that the library subsidizes the use of popular materials. Where there are multiple copies of high-use materials, it may well be appropriate to levy rental costs for the use of duplicate copies. The library enables its users to gain increased access to popular materials while permitting them to choose since it is still possible to place a reserve on the library's original copy.

POLICIES

All policies relating to the use of library materials should be prominently displayed at every circulation point. If they are complex, a handbook should be available. Unless these procedures are followed, users may be able to claim that they were unaware of the rules. This is also a reason for keeping these policies simple. If they are difficult to interpret, uncompliant users may claim that they were not informed about them. While this suggestion seems basic, many libraries do not inform users of their rights and responsibilities. Having the appropriate notices and a staff that is fully informed can prevent undesirable confrontations. Policies should be approved by the appropriate controlling body, whether the board of trustees, the local government, or the faculty senate and the administration. Nothing is more fruitless than trying to enforce procedures that have not been given such approval.

Some state statutes place the misuse or misappropriation of library materials within the provisions of their criminal codes. In such cases, it is appropriate to follow the proper legal procedures for the recovery of library materials, but there are also costs involved, and the library may wish to consider whether the results justify them. In all settings, community relations are important, and policies regarding such fees and fines should be structured to promote good relations. The goal is to ensure that all users have equal access to library materials. The measures used should promote this goal. Unless libraries keep this in mind, it is only too easy to develop policies that can discriminate against certain segments of the population.

NOTES

1. This is shown in Yvette Tilson's article "Income Generation and Pricing in Libraries," *Bottom Line* 8, no. 2 (1995): 23–26, which shows that fines for overdues are almost universal in the libraries studied. The same appears to be the case in the United States, but there are no definitive surveys available.

2. Robert Burgin and Patsy Hansel, "Library Overdues: An Update," *Library and Archival Security* 10, no. 2 (1990): 51–75.

3. "ULC Reports Most Members Without Fee-charging Policies, " *Library Journal* 118 (1 May 1993): 14–15.

4. "$172.58 Fine Dropped," *Hartford Courant*, 22 March 1996, A2.

5. Burgin and Hansel, p. 51.

6. Barbara L. Berman, "Videos in Public Libraries: Free or Fee?" *Public and School Libraries* (1994): 29–35.

7. "Superintendent's Book Tax Nixed by the School Board," *American Libraries* 26, no. 11 (Dec. 1995): 1091–1092.

Chapter 3

Cost Recovery for Photocopying and Printouts

Library users have shown a continuing desire to obtain printed versions of the materials they wish to use despite the innovations of the electronic age. These may originate from other printed resources—photocopying—or electronic resources—printout. In either case, libraries have to deal with the resultant costs, and most have decided to handle them differently. The copying of existing printed resources involves the patron and the library in copyright concerns and the right of fair use. These legal issues are beyond the scope of this work and are constantly changing, but they must nevertheless be taken into account by all libraries. Generally, materials borrowed on interlibrary loan cannot be copied without the consent of the lending library. This and similar issues will be addressed in the chapter on interlibrary loan and document delivery. The uses of electronic services addressed here are those relating to library-owned electronic sources, such as CD-ROMs and similar databases. Copyright charges for printouts from electronic services, such as CD-ROMs and full-text databases like LEXIS/NEXIS, OCLC's FirstSearch, or IAC's Expanded Academic Index, are generally covered by the licensing agreement entered into by the library or by a consortium; exceptions occur, however, and libraries must be careful in their interpretation of any vendor agreements. Depending on the outcome of negotiations between the interested parties, a user fee may emerge, either for consulting, downloading, or copying electronic publications.[1] It is not possible at this time to predict the outcome of these discussions, but they will certainly affect library policies and finance in the future.

Photocopying of print materials has been an option since the late 1920s. Printing from electronic sources is a recent development and there is not much information available to guide library managers in relation to cost recovery. Any copy service costs libraries in terms of equipment, supplies, and staffing, and librarians will have to make decisions about how to pay for these services. They must be concerned with whether their libraries can or should absorb the costs of providing those documents to an individual user. These decisions ultimately relate to a library's mission, though the final determination may also be influenced by its budget. Before deciding upon charging users, library managers should examine their options.

Copy Service Concerns

- Can the library absorb the cost of downloading or print-out, or must some or all of the cost be borne by the user?
- What is the relationship to the original supplier?
- Is such copying permitted under the terms of purchase or lease?

PHOTOCOPYING

Photocopying was originally valued as a means of preserving library materials and of sharing and exchanging scholarly information. Users, however, quickly saw the advantage of photocopying over making notes or manually copying the material. Public photocopy machines were introduced in the 1950s, and photocopying has become commonplace, even generating businesses solely devoted to copying material.[2] For many years libraries have provided photocopy machines that patrons can use to create paper copies of materials they want to consult. Sometimes this service is provided directly by the library, but in other cases the service is provided by a vendor on contract to the library or institution. The decision as to which route to follow may be determined by the volume of copying involved or by the capacity of the library to handle the need. Where the volume is high, or the controlling institution has made the decision, the service may be contracted out. All libraries must consider the most appropriate path of action, weighing their own needs with their concerns about the quality, speed, and cost of a copy service.[3] Maintaining a large-volume copy service is expensive. The machines need to be maintained, there are supplies to be considered, and there is always the question of replacing aging equipment, as well as the staff time required. For these reasons, most large libraries have decided to outsource photocopying. Even smaller libraries may participate in a shared service. Outsourcing also moves the library away from a commercial service and may thus help preserve its nonprofit status.

Who Runs the Service?

If a library decides to go with a commercial service, it has several choices. In some cases the commercial service and the library sign a contract, and the company provides the machines, decides what to charge, and gives a percentage of the profits back to the library. In other situations, the vendor pays a fee for space within the library and provides the equipment, maintenance, and supplies. In an academic library, photocopying may be under another unit such as business services, and the revenue will be retained in the library or institutional budget. In any case, staffing is a consideration. If staffing is provided solely by the vendor, the library can expect to receive a lower return. Even filling the printer cassettes with paper can prove to be a time-consuming activity for library staff, and libraries should weigh this manpower expense against the higher return provided by maintaining photocopy equipment themselves. Although the contract a library negotiates with a commercial vendor will determine the direct charges, the library can still negotiate for library benefits.

If the library decides to "go it alone," it has to take into account not only the ongoing but the amortized costs of replacing and servicing equipment. Providing a large-volume copy service is expen-

---

Figure 3.1 Checklist for Selecting a Commercial Photocopy Service

	Yes	No
Can some library copying still be free?	—	—
Are there free user cards for library staff?	—	—
Are there limits on such benefits?	—	—
Is there provision for discount user cards?	—	—
If the agreement provides for the return of a certain share of the profits, does this income go to		
The library?	—	—
The governing institution?	—	—
How much must the library do to maintain the service?		
Is the library required to police such matters as paper supply and toner?	—	—
Does the library collect and account for the money deposited by users?	—	—
Will the library receive a share of the profits if it does so?	—	—
Will the library be responsible for holding the cash overnight?	—	—

---

sive. The equipment needs to be purchased and maintained, supplies bought, aging equipment replaced, and staff involved constantly. Most libraries expect that the revenues generated from a copy service will cover most, if not all, of the costs associated with that service, and should consider both fixed and variable costs. Fixed costs include the purchase or lease of the machine, coin box, debit card reader, training, and equipment depreciation. These should be amortized over the expected life of the equipment. Variable costs depend on use, e.g., the number of copies made, and will include such items as toner, developer, paper, drum, and maintenance. They represent an ongoing expense and can be translated into a cost per copy. Unless the fees collected exceed variable costs, the service will run at a loss. Once revenues cover supplies, they can contribute to the initial outlay for equipment and its replacement.

A separate fund should be established for reserving income for these purposes. If this is not done, it is only too easy to merge different sources of income and then face the problem of finding funds to purchase new photocopying equipment.

Whether outsourcing or providing photocopy services, the library must determine how it will provide for its own internal needs. In many cases this is addressed by having an agreed-on amount of free photocopying from the vendor, in others by retaining some independent copying machines for staff use only. Either of these solutions may leave the library with additional costs.

Setting Charges

Whether the photocopy service is run by the library or by a commercial vendor, charging for copies is a commonly accepted practice.[4] Most fee-based services in libraries, such as photocopying and online searching, have an expense-based, direct cost-use relationship.[5] Photocopy services differ from simply making materials available to the borrower. They allow users to duplicate existing materials for their personal use and ownership, though it also benefits the library because noncirculating material is less likely to be stolen or mutilated.

Determining charges reflects decisions about the type of service provided. If a commercial service is involved, it will set the price based on its own business costs, and the library will negotiate its percentage. A commercial service may be able to offer a lower unit cost, particularly if it can offer bulk-use cards at a discount. If the library operates the service, it may not be able to offer either discounts or purchase in bulk. A commercial service may be able to operate by charging 5¢ per page, while the library running a parallel service may need to charge 10¢. Any library should also be aware of the competition offered by outside commercial services, such as Kinko's and others, which may be able to charge

Figure 3.2 Worksheets for Estimating Photocopying Costs

Fixed Costs	Cost	Expected Lifespan	Amortized Fixed Costs
Photocopier			
Coin box			
Debit card reader			
Staff training			
Totals			

Variable Costs	Amount	No. of Copies	Cost per Copy
Toner			
Developer			
Paper			
Drum			
Maintenance			
Totals			

Gross Revenue	Amount
Minus Variable Costs	
Minus Amortized Fixed Costs	
Net Revenue	

a lower rate. The user will have little incentive to use the service in the library when an outside vendor can offer cheaper and possibly faster service.

Self-service or Staffed Centers?

Libraries will also need to make decisions about whether to offer self-service copiers, a staffed center, or a mixture of both options. While self-service areas are convenient for both the library and the user, staff will still be needed to monitor equipment and supplies. One disadvantage of self-service areas is that the library user may not be careful with the equipment, with resulting increased maintenance needs. Badly managed copying can also destroy important materials. In addition there is the possibility of vandalism in areas without staffing. Staffed centers are particularly common in microform areas, in part because these machines are more expensive and difficult to use, but also because it may be difficult to match a printing machine with the particular microform. Larger libraries, with substantial internal photocopying needs may want to provide both self- and staff-service centers, while a small library, with little demand for photocopying, may have a central location where a staff person makes copies. There is a trend in academic libraries to place staffed service centers under units such as business services. Financially, the supporting institution may require this kind of consolidation; this decision also addresses copyright concerns, since a separate unit will operate under different legal rules and may be able to provide some services the library itself cannot.

Management Concerns

The preceding discussions raise issues.

> ### Considerations in Organizing Photocopy Services
>
> - Determining the rates for service
>
> - Equipment problems
>
> - Holding cash for coin operated machines, debit machines, and money changers
>
> - Staffing—both self-service and library staffed locations
>
> - Placement of machines
>
> - Profitability of service
>
> - Vandalism

These concerns have been reported on by an American Library Association committee, an Association of Research Libraries study, and others.[6] There is little consensus, although it is clear that the problems and the need to find acceptable solutions are recognized.

It is clear, even from this short discussion of a very complex topic, that it is not simply a matter of setting up photocopy machines in the library and establishing copy charges. While it may not be possible to provide free photocopying to library users, the library must provide the best service it can at the best price.[7]

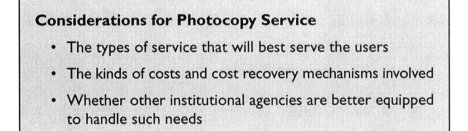

> ### Considerations for Photocopy Service
>
> - The types of service that will best serve the users
>
> - The kinds of costs and cost recovery mechanisms involved
>
> - Whether other institutional agencies are better equipped to handle such needs

The library must decide whether to provide the service from its resources and determine the charges to be levied or to outsource the service, negotiating a contract that serves both the library and its users. Outsourcing may not be an option in smaller communities, in which case the library must undertake the task itself, setting prices in accordance with its costs. In larger communities outsourcing may be the best option, and the contract must be set to provide the maximum benefits both to the user and to the library. Outsourcing always involves two questions: Is this the best way to provide a local service? and, Could this be done better by the library itself? There are no ready answers. In some settings local service will prove more beneficial, in others service by an outside provider. The larger the volume the more likely that a commercial entity can provide better service. This can place smaller communities at a disadvantage, hence the interest in collective or shared services, such as can be developed within a consortium.

PRINTOUTS

Like photocopies, printouts provide individuals with a personal copy of material that does not circulate, belongs to someone else, or is otherwise available only electronically. Most users do not want simply to view or read material on a screen, but to have copies that they can carry with them, mark up, and read at their leisure. While libraries are primarily interested in access, users are often interested in ownership. This concept was emphasized by several of the speakers at the 1996 Charleston Conference. It was suggested that it might well be one reason why the electronic publication of entire books would be delayed, since either downloading or printing hundreds of pages is a slow and expensive process. Short articles or entries from encyclopedias are not nearly as costly to reproduce. This difference is often overlooked in general discussions of what library services are needed, how it will relate to interlibrary loan, and what resultant charges can be levied.

Background

Computers at first seemed to promise a paperless society, as was once suggested after the advent of microforms, and few people anticipated the amount of paper that would be consumed by printing computerized products. Demands for paper have actually increased with growing availability of electronic information. Ten years ago, for example, librarians carried out online searches for users and printed information selectively; there was a limited amount of information in electronic format, and database searching required specialized training. Today, users frequently perform searches themselves and print whatever they want. A recent instance, when one of the authors was visiting another library, was the sight of a student printing out hundreds of citations from the online catalog, using three printers in the process, because the downloading software was not working. The result was three thick stacks of paper. How much of that would really be useful is difficult to estimate, but it demonstrates that simply because they can do it, many people will print out anything they have access to. Printing has become a whole new concept in information retrieval.

Printing is a fairly new concern for libraries, and there is little information available and no apparent consistency in policies or procedures. While discussions of printing are popular on the Internet, there is very little in the published literature—articles heralding the virtual library rarely mention it.[8] The only study published at the time of preparation of this chapter was a 1992 report of printing in ARL libraries.[9] At that time, seven libraries charged for public printing, thirty-seven were considering charging, and eleven were discussing it. Printing of this kind was certainly not a prime consideration when libraries began investigating and adding electronic resources. Most libraries began with one or two computer terminals, sometimes with attached printers. Users most often printed a few citations or call numbers and took the printout with them. Printing was small-scale and manageable. Gradually, libraries added more computers, databases (particularly full-text), and printers. A good example is the Sterling Library at Yale University, where the many terminals accessing the catalog also access databases, word processing services, and printers, changing the area from collection-directed to general use. Library managers have begun to realize that they are spending thousands of dollars on printing and that these costs will probably escalate. It is still not clear, however, how these costs relate to library objectives and whether there should be any attempt to recover them.

It is increasingly apparent that libraries must reconsider charging for printing in much the same way as they had to reexamine photocopying. Can the library afford the costs of printing articles, electronic books, Internet documents with graphics available through graphical browsers (i.e., Netscape, Mosaic), and similar products likely to be generated in the future? What is the cost of paper, ribbons, or toner? A library with many electronic resources and printers can spend a considerable amount of money: in the summer of 1996 a ream of paper (500 pages) cost between $3.00 and $5.00, and a laser cartridge $90.00. A library can easily spend $150.00 a week ($7,800.00 a year) for printouts from a single printer.

Arguments for Charging

Librarians are excited, and rightly so, about the new electronic technologies and the potential of increased access to information. They concentrate on selecting appropriate sources, making them available, promoting their use, and instructing patrons how to use and evaluate these information resources. Printing is an afterthought, a convenience for the user, and, compared to many of the electronic services, costs appear negligible. Given the reality of budget constraints, librarians should examine carefully whether or not they need to charge a fee, at least for some printouts. Like other decisions about charging for a library service, this one will ultimately depend on the individual library and its governing authority, mission, and clientele. Printouts present a private rather than a public good: because users have access to the information without printing it out, the printout benefits the individual, not the public in general. It may also be difficult to justify charging for printouts of call numbers and citations with no guarantee that the book is currently available or that the library owns the periodical. However, when the information is full-text, a printout provides the user with a personal copy. The library should consider charging, and most users will understand that it may be an extraordinary service for which they should pay a fee.

Printing represents an additional, unpredictable expense for a library. It is as unreasonable to assume that the library should support the costs associated with unlimited printouts as to believe that it should provide unlimited, free photocopying. If the library does not recover at least part of its costs, it will need to find supplemental funds or forego other purchases or services. Charging may also help to control overuse. Users may be unaware of the actual cost associated with printouts and thus request an excessive number of printouts if there are no financial restraints. Overuse can also occur when patrons are not trained to use the system properly. When printers are networked the user may not realize that a printout has been activated and may repeat the same search several times. He or she may even print one call number (two lines) per page on a laser printer. The hurried user may be tempted to print and evaluate later. Students, for example, have been known to print articles in German and French, even though they could not read these languages. Charging for printouts provides incentives for learning to use the system correctly and efficiently. The library may also unknowingly encourage users to evaluate information sources on cost and ease of access rather than quality and relevance if it charges for one, photocopies for example, and not another.

Why Charge for Printouts?

- Represents an extraordinary library service
- Recovers at least some of the costs involved
- Helps control overuse
- Maintains consistency among formats

DETERMINING FEES AND METHODS OF COLLECTION

Librarians often do not know what is actually being spent for printing. The costs may well be buried in the general budget within several different budget items as few libraries keep the costs of public printing separated from those for staff printing or interlibrary loan. There is little consistency in pricing, and most libraries appear to charge an arbitrary amount. In the 1992 study of ARL libraries, charges ranged from 5¢ to 35¢ per page.[10] In order to set accurate and reasonable fees, librarians should consider the charges assessed for printouts, photocopies, and other print services at other venues, including an academic computing center or a commercial business such as a copy service or bookstore. The sophistication and cost of the library's equipment will also figure into decisions on printout fees. Format, the ease with which printouts are accomplished, and the configuration of computers and printers will be important considerations (see the section on "Equipment Considerations" in this chapter).

The library must also determine how payment will be accepted. Libraries with a few workstations and attached printers may have a debit card or coin-operated machine attached to the printer so that the user pays before receiving the printout. Networked systems present greater difficulties. Some libraries have an honor system, with users paying at a central location, others have users download information and print at another station that has an attached printer that requires payment. Another option is to direct the printout to a high-speed printer in a central, staffed area and have the user pay before picking it up. Billable user accounts may be suitable for an academic library. Building such accounts for outside users, however, may be difficult for a public library. Charges may also be collected through a technology fee (increasingly common in academic institutions) or a membership fee suitable for outside users. Special software that sends the print request to a computer dedicated as a print server that directs the printout to a laser printer is a recent innovation. The user leaves the first workstation, identifies and pays for the printout, and then prints. While this solution has potential, it may also result in long lines of users waiting for printouts, causing confusion in a busy library. It also requires the user to plan his or her needs carefully in order to avoid multiple trips to the printer.

Regardless of the collection method, payment should be as easy as possible. Both change and card machines should be readily found in a central location: if there are several floors, machines will be needed on each floor that has the appropriate printers. To accommodate both the regular and the occasional user, machines should accept both coins and debit cards. Where there are several machines in one location, some may handle only cash, to pro-

Collecting Fees

Collection possibilities:

- honor system
- debit card or coin-operated machine attached to the printer
- output sent to a print server that is attached to a networked printer with a charge machine
- output sent to a centralized, staffed location
- users given individual accounts and billed for use (i.e., through a student's account)
- users charged through a technology or membership fee

vide for the casual or outside user, while the others accept both cards and cash. Many colleges and universities have implemented systems which allow the student or faculty card to be used as a debit card.

In deciding which change and card machines to use, the library should consider what denominations of currency will be accepted. Users often complain if they are required to bring the correct change, even when that is a dollar bill. Changers that accept bills in larger denominations return silver dollars, and users then need to find another machine that makes change for those dollars. Users often want change for telephone calls, bus fares, metered parking, photocopies, and other needs in addition. It is sound fiscal policy not to have staff make change, except perhaps at the circulation desk where they are handling fines and similar charges. If this is not done, it may be very difficult to reconcile cash records.

Equipment Considerations

Although most libraries are automated, there is a good deal of variation in the way the associated technologies are configured. One library may have only an online catalog, another may have an online catalog together with one or two CD-ROM stations with

	Yes	No
Figure 3.3 Checklist for Setting Photocopying and Printing Charges		
Is the library interested in recovering costs or controlling overuse?	—	—
Can the library determine the costs of printing?	—	—
What type(s) of printing carry charges?		
Printouts from the OPAC?	—	—
Printouts of citations?	—	—
Printouts of full-text articles?	—	—
Printouts of books?	—	—
Does the staff have guidelines for charging?	—	—
Are there allowances for exceptions?	—	—
What methods of payment are possible?		
Cash?	—	—
Debit cards?	—	—
Are change machines easily available?	—	—

attached printers, and yet another may have many databases (both citation-based and full-text) and computers networked to laser printers. Libraries can expect to be even more highly automated in the future and need to begin establishing guidelines now rather than waiting until the situation has become a problem. Unless this proactive view is taken, the library risks always being behind the times. The decisions made in updating and maintaining its electronic technology will influence the library's fees for the use of such services and their outputs.

Unfortunately, there is little consistency in protocol among the various electronic products. Each vendor has developed its own procedures for printing. As libraries acquire access to different databases and vendors, users may need to learn a variety of print commands. In some systems, for example, users mark or tag records and then push the F4 key; in others they may need to load

Figure 3.4 Worksheet for Forecasting Information Technology Needs

Item or Equipment	Current Number	In Two Years	In Five Years
OPAC Terminals			
Stand-alone workstations			
Networked workstations			
Citation-based databases			
Full-text databases			
E-journals			
Internet Stations			
Browser Stations (Netscape, Mosaic, etc.)			
Dot matrix printers			
Laser printers			
Other (e.g., color printers)			

records into a log file and print later. There are many other variations. The resulting confusion and frustration leads to stress for librarian and user alike. Library managers will need to evaluate the ease with which a printout can be accomplished and the monetary value of such convenience. The type(s) of printers selected and their configurations will also affect charging. Many libraries, for example, have dot matrix printers with tractor-fed paper. Users print what they need and tear off the paper. Other libraries have installed ink, jet, or laser printers that print one page at a time. These printing systems are very different, and the response times are also different, which makes the computation of charges difficult. A further issue is the way in which computers and printers are linked.

Network Configuration

- Is printing capacity available at every workstation?

- Are there stand-alone workstations with attached printers or printers shared by two or more workstations?

- Is the shared printer in the immediate area or in a centralized, staffed location, such as the circulation or the reference desk?

These are important questions, and the library manager may not be aware of their impact before installing a networked printer. When a workstation has an attached printer it is relatively easy to link the requester with the print request; it is only slightly more difficult when two workstations share a single printer. When printers are networked, however, one printer serves several computer terminals and the print requests go into a single print queue. Special procedures will then be needed to identify the user with the print request. The alternative is massive confusion when the user asks for his or her printout.

SPECIAL SERVICES

Brief mention was made earlier in this chapter of special needs relating to photocopying. In some instances, the condition of the material, its rarity (e.g., special collections), or special circumstances such as illustrations and diagrams require a procedure other than simple user-initiated photocopying. While many libraries do not have the capacity to handle such special needs, others run their own reproduction services and can handle these requests. Regular reproduction systems are not always well equipped to handle color illustrations (though this situation is improving), extensive diagrams, poor original copies, or large pages. The handling of fragile materials also requires special care. Some vendors have produced photocopy machines structured to handle bound volumes, but there are many other alternatives. Some libraries, for example Penn State, have outsourced this kind of service, because other agencies are better equipped to handle it. Others have their own photocopy service units for handling unusual projects. This may be particularly true where the library itself is engaged in endeavors such as digitization or preservation or has an internal, specialized bindery as is the case with Johns Hopkins. The costs can be quite high, and the library is justified in imposing commensurate charges. What those charges should be has to relate to the cost of providing the service. Again, it is not a question of whether the request is permissible under copyright guidelines—which must be determined separately—but of what charges should be levied for the process of reproduction and any royalty payments involved.

Both these settings apply to materials supplied by other libraries, whether through interlibrary loan or document delivery. A request for photocopies of another institution's materials involves operational costs that the library is entitled to recover. These will be discussed at more length in the chapter on interlibrary loan and document delivery. Some libraries impose a standard cost, plus per page charges over a certain number of pages. This is a logical way to proceed, because setting up the photocopying procedure involves administrative costs, justifying an up-front fee. Some libraries, for instance, levy a base cost of $15–25.00 simply to provide photocopying up to a stated number of pages. The same costs may or may not be charged to the library's own users; if the service has been outsourced, however, a similar charge is likely.

Even more appropriate would be the recovery of the costs of downloading and printing material from electronic sources through a fee-based service. The question is whether this kind of service is free, subject to a fee, or subsidized, even if only for a certain class of user, e.g., students.[11] The resultant fees could include not only the direct cost of printing but also the indirect cost of the labor required to locate and recover the materials needed, plus any charges levied by the original supplier. In all such settings, copyright implications must be considered. Libraries must behave like any other document supplier and pass on any charges to the individual user. The best course is to establish a base cost, e.g., $10.00, then add any other direct costs involved. As the amount of electronic information increases so will user demands to print anything they find on the Internet. Here one must also realize that, although it seems relatively easy to recover listservs and the like from the Internet, their reproductive quality is not high and may need enhancement, not always possible for the individual library. Libraries should not seek to compete with other printing services but can anticipate that users will want to print graphics, even in color, and some libraries might want to consider providing high-resolution and/or color printers and adjusting their charges accordingly.

While libraries have long been in the business of providing access to information, this has traditionally been accomplished by purchasing, cataloging, and lending library materials. The collection was in-house, and most of it could be checked out to individuals. Items that did not circulate could be copied, either by hand or by a photocopy machine. In the future, much information will be available only electronically, and users may not be able physically to check out individual items. However, they can still copy them, either by hand or by printouts. Most users have accepted the legitimacy of charges for photocopy and will probably do so for printouts. At this time, charging for printouts is somewhat difficult to manage because the publishing and copying industries have not yet developed an easy method for collecting charges, whether royalties or internal library costs. A uniform system will, however, come, probably in the near future. The decision may cause a further reconsideration of library procedures, since it may be necessary to link much more closely with such institutions as the Copyright Clearance Center or to respond directly to publisher charges.

NOTES

1. This is an interpretation of reports of the Green and White papers on *Intellectual Property and the National Information Infrastructure*, prepared by the Information Infrastructure Taskforce and presented to the Department of Commerce as part of the negotiations for revising the Copyright Act. Discussions continue and so far have not presented an agreement between the parties involved in the Conference on Fair Use (CONFU) discussions.

2. For a more complete discussion of the history of photocopiers, see William Z. Nazri, "Reprography," in *Encyclopedia of Library and Information Science,* ed. Allen Kent, Harold Lancour, and Jay E. Daly (New York: Marcel Dekker, 1978), 230–239.

3. Raize Dorr, "Planning Photocopy Services: A Success Story," *Bottom Line* 3, no. 1 (1989): 22.

4. The Washington state attorney general challenged the Seattle Public Library's plan to charge fees for electronic services but not for photocopying, which was described as an "ancillary service." "News in Brief," *American Libraries* 25, no. 4 (May 1993): 377.

5. Philip M. Ray, "Information Economics and Libraries in the Digital Age," *Bottom Line* 9, no. 2 (1996): 30.

6. American Library Association. Reproduction of Library Materials Section. Photocopying Costs in Libraries Committee. Reproduction of Library Materials Committee, "Report of the Photocopying Costs in Libraries Committee," *Library Resources & Technical Services* 14, no. 2 (1970): 279–289; *Photocopy Services in ARL Libraries* (Washington, D. C.: ARL Systems and Procedures Exchange Center, 1985) (SPEC Kit 115); Scott Finet, "Options in Offering a Photocopy Service," *The Bottom Line* 5, no. 3 (1991): 18–24.

7. David C. Taylor, "Serials Management: Issues and Recommendations," in *Issues in Library Management: A Reader for the Professional Librarian* (White Plains, N. Y.: Knowledge Industry Publications), 82–96.

8. A search through the 1996 issues of *College & Research Libraries, Computers in Libraries, Information Technology and Libraries, Library Hi-Tech, Library Hi-Tech News*, and *Library Administration and Management* yielded no mention of printing.

9. Suzanne Taylor and C. Brigid Welch, ed., *Provision of Computer Printing Capabilities to Library Patrons* (Washington, D. C.: Association of Research Libraries, Systems and Procedures Exchange Center, 1992). (SPEC Kit 183)

10. Taylor and Welch, p. 5.

11. William L. Whitson, "The Way I See It: Fee, Free, or Subsidy? The Future Role of Libraries," *College & Research Library News* 55, no. 7 (July–August, 1994): 426–427.

Chapter 4

Interlibrary Loan and Document Delivery

Because any one library is unlikely to be able to satisfy all of its user needs, libraries have developed systematic responses to enable users to consult unowned materials. The traditional response has been interlibrary loan, whereby libraries (not individual users) could gain access to needed materials. These are transactions between libraries, not between individuals, a distinction important in terms of the prevailing copyright legislation (there may be some changes in future, pending legislation). The increasing complexity of the information market has introduced a second response— document delivery. Although there are similarities between these services, the differences are even more significant. This chapter looks at these differences and similarities and how they should be handled. It is almost certain that many, if not most, libraries will in the future operate both services because they serve different needs. There is no suggestion here that one may supplant the other, only that each will operate within its own defined sphere, responding to the possibilities, needs, and financial constraints of each kind of service.

Interlibrary loan is a contract between libraries, not between individuals, while document delivery is a personal transaction whereby a library endeavors to provide materials to an individual user, based on the economic premises of supply and demand. This difference is becoming blurred as libraries realize the true cost of meeting user demands. Is it simply a matter of enabling the user to consult materials the library does not own, or of providing materials for the individual user's benefit? Borrowing an entire book may simply be a substitute for library ownership and circulation; asking for entire articles or other kinds of documents that the library would not normally have purchased is a murkier issue. Lending collectively is somewhat different from making copies available for reading, even if those copies are made under fair use provisions. Lending is a transaction between libraries; document delivery usually involves a third party, whether publisher or commercial vendor. The former is an extension of the First Sale Doctrine, the latter a transaction governed by other components of copyright, contract, and commercial law.

Libraries need to distinguish carefully between interlibrary loan and document delivery on an organizational basis. There are both legal and economic considerations, but libraries must take into account what best meets the user's need. The shift towards viewing information as a commercial good has altered the lines between the two kinds of transactions. In the rush to avail themselves of the benefits of online services, many libraries have failed to distinguish between what is permissible under copyright law and what must be paid for as a commercial transaction. Unless these distinctions are recognized, libraries and their users may find themselves paying more than they should for information. Any library undertaking document delivery should take care to see that it does not intermingle with interlibrary loan, even if only at the level of keeping separate records and keeping the cash transactions separate. A full examination of these issues can be found in *Access Versus Assets*, by Barbra Higginbotham and Sally Bowdoin,[1] which is essential reading for all librarians involved in either interlibrary loan or document delivery.

INTERLIBRARY LOAN

Interlibrary loan is based on the willingness of libraries to share materials owned. The manner of sharing is governed by national and regional codes, and may be affected by consortial and similar agreements, but the basic concept is that libraries and users all gain by the ability to consult and read materials that are not owned locally. In terms of monographs and other self-contained publications, this kind of transaction does not impinge on copyright and similar proprietorial issues, and will probably continue indefinitely because of the time, cost, and difficulties associated with copying or downloading entire volumes. Another factor, not always recognized, is that tracking down obscure publications requires full professional skills and cannot be left to clerical interpretation of computerized records. Access to articles and other subsets of publications becomes less clear. The Copyright Act of 1976 confirmed the right of fair use, and the National Commission on Technological Uses of Copyrighted Works (CONTU) guidelines, developed from the Congressional hearings involved, suggested rules and limits for library use. Books and similar items can be lent between libraries but cannot be copied. While entire publications cannot be copied (including complete poems, maps, diagrams, and the like), other than for personal use, libraries can provide photocopied articles in lieu of sending the actual publication. Borrowing libraries must be continually aware of the suggested limits. It is also important to realize that it may be more prudent financially to subscribe to a periodical than to pay commercial delivery or interlibrary loan charges for several individual articles. In one instance cited in an e-mail letter, the cost of individual articles far exceeded subscription fees.[2] This runs counter to the present trend of cancelling subscriptions to reduce library costs on the assumption that the direct ordering of individual articles will always be cheaper. This situation has to be taken into consideration when deciding who pays for what services. It may seem simpler just to charge the user for individual articles, but it is also possible that both the library and its user community might stand to benefit from a subscription. The present is not always the most reliable guide to the future.

Behind the use of interlibrary loan lies the idea that libraries are furthering the sharing of knowledge, a prime objective stated in U. S. copyright legislation. It is a method which, if not costless, may at least be less costly than buying the materials in question. Despite the example cited above of the cost of borrowing several articles from one journal, the more usual situation is a once in a lifetime need for a specific book or article. Numerous studies have shown that there is a very real cost,[3] not only for the borrowing library but for the lending library as well. The costs will vary library by library and are affected by any number of consortial or state-supported programs. Before the development of electronic information systems and the recent advent of commercial document delivery services, interlibrary loan seemed to be the only way to obtain needed materials that were not owned by the library. In that setting, it seemed inequitable to charge users for obtaining materials the library had not purchased—in a way making up for a library failure. The same argument has been applied to cancelled serial titles and has also often been backed up by a fund created from recovered expenditures from cancelled subscriptions to subsidize subsequent borrowing or photocopy purchase. Not all libraries have been in a position to follow this route. If they cannot subsidize their users, should they then charge them for materials borrowed on their behalf? Earlier the answer would have been, certainly not, but fiscal reality is changing that response, which was never entirely true anyway.

Now that budgets have become tighter, many libraries have begun to question interlibrary loan's status as a free service, and at the very least are thinking of recovering some of the out-of-pocket costs involved. The RLG/ARL study clearly showed that interlibrary loan is an expensive way of providing materials for users.[4] To a certain degree, this cost is levelled by the mutual nature of interlibrary loan. Each participant gives and receives, and ultimately the costs and benefits tend to cancel one another out. This is particularly true within small consortia. Nevertheless, interlibrary loan is still a costly service for individual, rather than collective, benefit. Most libraries have begun to consider whether there should be cost recovery, either internally or externally.[5] In the first case, libraries charge their users, either fully or partially, for a special service. In the second, libraries charge other libraries for the use of their resources. Some libraries have for a considerable time levied substantial charges on outside users, partly as a deterrent against overuse, but also to recover costs incurred. For the most part, these have been major research libraries, which due to their scholarly reputation were often approached because of the presumption rather than the knowledge that they owned the needed materials.

Access to increasingly universal databases, such as OCLC or RLIN, has reduced that problem to some degree, but the fact remains that some libraries will always be targeted for interlibrary loan and others named as resource libraries within a state system. State, regional, and other cooperatives have helped to reduce this kind of dependence, but within any group there will always be net lender and net borrower libraries. The resolution of this kind of imbalance will be addressed more fully in chapter six. Any library may examine the worth of a prohibitive or cost recovery fee if its services are being overused. This consideration was built directly into the New Zealand scheme of interloan, which once presumed the maintenance of a balance between lending and borrowing, that seems to expect and accept a scheme of charges for service.[6] The goal remains the balancing of lending and borrowing, with the added recognition that libraries may have to recover their costs. Incidentally, libraries that are not full members (i.e., borrowers and lenders) of the New Zealand interloan may face further charges and certainly agree to pay any charges levied.

While academic libraries have seldom imposed a direct user fee for interlibrary loan requests, public libraries have often considered them a service beyond their statutory duties and have developed a system of fees. The charges imposed are generally minimal ($5.00 or $10.00), but they do help recover the costs involved in providing personal services. The difference in approach between academic and public libraries can be assigned to the difference in their missions. Academic libraries are presumed to advance scholarship and act on behalf of their communities in this purpose. Public libraries provide general support of community needs and cannot cope with the added costs of providing special individual services. Special libraries lie uneasily in the middle. They will always need materials they do not have, and even though they may be able to recover costs from departmental budgets or client accounts, there is often no ready budget mechanism to provide support for such activities. Moreover, they will always tend to be net borrowers. In these circumstances many special libraries prefer to deal with a fee-based document delivery service rather than the interlibrary loan unit. This suggests an increasing divergence between the two kinds of services, particularly in their target markets.

To judge from an increasing number of policy documents and cost recovery policies, many libraries are moving toward some kind of fee-based interlibrary loan. Libraries have shown little compunction in recovering the costs incurred in document delivery, possibly because they are so readily identifiable. Why should interlibrary loan be any different?[7] The costs incurred by lending and borrowing libraries are no different in essence from the costs incurred by a commercial firm. While they are not incurred with a view to making a profit, library costs would not otherwise have to be met. On the other hand, interlibrary loan depends on the cooperation of libraries nation- and world-wide, which implies some kind of understanding about shared responsibilities and costs. It is, however, quite possible that interlibrary loan will develop into a nearly universal fee-based system because it will be reduced to dealing with the difficult needs that could not be addressed by document delivery, thus becoming a very costly service that would be used only when there was no other alternative.

The issue here is balancing a private (personal) good against a public (community or institutional) good. Should the library subsidize or pay for personal goods? William Whitson has presented a first exploration of this issue in academic libraries,[8] suggesting that a subsidy is a reasonable concept but that direct costs should not simply be absorbed by the library. In any event, unless the entire cost, direct and indirect, of each transaction is recovered, there will always be an element of subsidy. Libraries have been slow to recognize the need to recover indirect costs except in the case of fee-based services, but they must be taken into account when operating a document delivery service. Sometimes institutional goals cloud the issue. In a university, research may be perceived as an institutional goal. In a corporate library, added information may forward corporate goals. In a public library, personal study could benefit the community, e.g., causing wider local employment; nevertheless, it is clear that one person (individual or corporate) is the primary benefactor. Balancing these needs and benefits is like walking a tightrope. If libraries provide all such services free, they can find themselves absorbing a great many costs for activities that do not benefit the general population. If, on the other hand, they levy charges or recover costs, they may be defeating their own informational purposes. The resolution of this situation depends on the ability of the supporting institution or community to provide the necessary budget for the operation. Caught in this dilemma, libraries must develop policies that determine how they will respond to personal requests for information not owned by the library. These policies are not always simple to establish, since they may depend on the decisions of other libraries, a state library, or a consortium.

Should Libraries Charge for Interlibrary Loan?

This issue has existed for many years. If access to information is a basic library goal, the answer appears to be no, but libraries also have to consider how best to use their limited financial resources. How far can they go in ensuring that users find the information they need when it is not owned locally? Borrowing materials from other libraries can be an expensive process, but obtaining them through commercial sources can be even more costly. It is likely, therefore, that there will be some element of cost recovery in either transaction.

BASE CHARGES

Few academic or special libraries impose a basic charge on their own patrons for interlibrary loan, presumably because the service helps forward their basic goals. Public libraries, however, often see interlibrary loan as an added-value service that justifies a basic fee. Given the willingness of libraries to charge for document delivery services, reluctance to charge for interlibrary loan may seem implausible; there are differences, however. An entire book cannot be duplicated through document delivery, but there are many instances where fair use and similar legal doctrines avoid the application of royalties and similar assessments. It is consequently possible to argue that there are two kinds of interlibrary loan that need not be subject to the same rules: one that deals with materials that are not subject to copyright and another that does. Whatever the case, there are library costs involved, and these are what basic charges seek to recover in part or in whole. Another possibility is to levy a basic charge on a requesting library. As mentioned earlier, this may function as either a deterrent or a cost recovery mechanism. The existence of cooperative agreements may exclude some external users from fees. The more complex such arrangements are, the more time consuming it becomes to determine the best solution to any individual request; moreover, the calculation and payment of such reciprocal costs may become a major cost element.

The level of fee charged, if any, should reflect the added value of the service. A purely nominal fee looks more like a deterrent and does not recover the actual cost. Charges should at least cover the out-of-pocket costs, such as postage, and recover some staff costs. Given the apparent cost of providing interlibrary loan, a fee of at least $10.00 seems reasonable, but the actual amount charged should be determined by the political and financial circumstances of the library.

COST RECOVERY CHARGES

For a regular loan of a book or similar item, the costs involved are primarily postage charges; they may also include any other charges levied by the lending library, for example, the cost of recovering the item. Given that the benefit is private, it is legitimate to recover such costs. Be aware, however, that the accounting costs associated with any such transaction are significant. For many years, interlibrary loan departments sent one another stamps to cover postage, but records were rarely kept, to the dismay of the auditors. If a complete record of such transactions is required, the costs of keeping it will rapidly outweigh the income received. There is no simple answer to this dilemma. The postage incurred by a lending library has to be recovered from the borrowing library, rather than from the individual user. Lest this seem to be a minor matter, it should be remembered that international interlibrary loan may well involve substantial postal fees. If libraries transfer sums of money, there will be bank charges as well. For these reasons, many libraries have entered into cooperative agreements, understanding that individual library costs tend to cancel one another out. Any problems may be resolved by a kind of group accounting that results in a single balancing payment or by an agreement to absorb local costs. States may also provide funds to support net lending libraries. OCLC has developed an accounting system to record interinstitutional expenditures that could simplify individual library recordkeeping, but it is important to note that some libraries operate within several lending systems and not all their costs could be so recorded. The OCLC system is well described in *Access Versus Assets*.[9]

OTHER COSTS

Lending a book or similar unique item is a relatively simple transaction. Supplying photocopies or microform copies are more complicated transactions. Quite apart from any legal considerations, the library has to consider the cost of copying an article or of making a microform copy of the material required. In the same way as libraries have found it impossible to provide free photocopying to internal users, it is unlikely that they can continue to provide free copies through interlibrary loan. It is reasonable to expect that libraries will want to be compensated for making such copies. The charges involved should relate to the cost of internal photocopying, but also take into account that it is the library staff rather than the individual user who must recover and copy the needed materials. For this reason, libraries have tended to establish charges that relate to the amount of photocopying required.[10] The best way of doing this is to set a minimum charge, adding additional costs that reflect the amount of copying involved. This can be done by setting charges that add page costs beyond an initial amount. The same rationale applies to making microform copies of materials; the charges may be greater, however, reflecting the larger costs involved. Several guides to interlibrary loan policies are available, but it has to be kept in mind that these policies are continually changing.[11]

DOCUMENT DELIVERY

As distinct from interlibrary loan, document delivery is a quasi-commercial service. It is a transaction between the library and an individual, mostly using commercial services as the delivery agents rather than other libraries. It is consequently appropriate that the usual commercial rules for charges be applied. For a library this is particularly important, because delivery services, even those provided by libraries such as the British Library Document Delivery

---

Figure 4.1 Checklist for Establishing Cost Recovery in Interlibrary Loan: Borrowing

	Yes	No
Is there a basic charge per transaction?	—	—
Does this charge apply to all borrowers?	—	—
Is there a differential charge for nonmembers?	—	—
Is the intention to cover all costs?	—	—
Or only partial costs?	—	—
Will the library pass on out-of-pocket costs?	—	—
Photocopy charges?	—	—
Postal charges?	—	—
Rush charges?	—	—
Recordkeeping costs?	—	—
Other lending library charges?	—	—

Centre, expect to recover their expenses, including royalty payments, photocopying costs, and postage. The operational costs of the business involved will also be included. In all cases service claims of commercial firms have to be weighed against the regular alternative of interlibrary loan. Many such firms have made a big pitch for their quicker response time, even though that does not always occur in practice. Others have built their services on existing publications, e.g., ISI and *Current Contents*. Some, such as UnCover Inc., combine library and commercial expertise. Does the firm in question claim to be able to access any information anywhere, or are there limits as to what it will cover? The wider the reach the more likely it will be that the service will be more expensive. It is also important to recognize that most commercial services have constraints as to what they can or cannot provide and that entire books are unlikely service objectives; then some complex materials and time-consuming transactions will continue to be the responsibility of interlibrary loan. Additionally, most commercial services still depend on library collections as sources, and

---

**Figure 4.2 Checklist for Establishing Cost Recovery in
Interlibrary Loan: Lending**

	Yes	No
Is there a basic charge per transaction?	—	—
Does this include postage?	—	—
Does this include document recovery charges?	—	—
Or, are these supplemental charges?	—	—
Is there a basic charge for photocopying?	—	—
Set sum up to a given number of pages?	—	—
Is there a page charge?	—	—
Is this progressive?	—	—
Is there a limit to the number of pages?	—	—
Is there a maximum charge?	—	—
Is there a charge for record-keeping?	—	—
Is there a cooperative accounting arrangement?	—	—
Is there a fund for reimbursing net lenders?	—	—
Can credit cards be used?	—	—
Personal?	—	—
Corporate?	—	—
Departmental?	—	—

---

those libraries may feel justified in establishing charges for such a service, which will then be passed on to users.

Often, libraries have entered the document delivery business themselves because budget cuts have affected their ability to purchase subscriptions.[12] Others attempt to combine interlibrary loan and document delivery to provide a completer service and recover some of their costs.[13] It is indeed likely that libraries will find themselves in a setting not unlike individual entrepreneurs, whose costs rise as they seek to respond to the more esoteric of their users' demands. In this situation, libraries may feel justified in recovering their full costs for interlibrary loan service, even while they provide a parallel document delivery service.

Document Delivery and the Library's Nonprofit Status

Libraries that undertake document delivery service must recognize that they are also entering a commercial arena and the resulting charges will reflect the use of firms that have to cover their costs of operation. In many instances the result may well be cost-beneficial, but libraries must then determine how, or if, they will recover their own expenditures. This leads inevitably to a cost-benefit evaluation and the establishment of a fee-based service that runs like a business. Consequently, libraries undertaking this kind of service will have to determine its effects upon their nonprofit status. It may be desirable to set up a document delivery service as a profit center, separate from regular library operations in much the same way as a fee-based service. This relates to the status of the library as a public entity, rather than profitmaking. If library overheads are not taken into account, it is indeed likely that the status of the operation will be called into question by the Internal Revenue Service. This is a further reason why libraries should be more concerned with the total financial picture than with individual operations.

Cost Recovery

Regardless of decisions about status, libraries will have to decide what costs to recover and how to charge for them. Should all costs, both direct and indirect, be recovered, or only direct, out-of-pocket costs? The first decision places the document delivery service directly in the commercial sector. The second raises the question of whether there is any difference between document delivery and interlibrary loan and why a separate service was set up. The reconsideration of copyright issues resulting from the establishment of the Internet and publishers' reactions to the use of electronic materials make the question of difference a financial issue.[14] Downloading electronic publications can be very expensive and will almost certainly include royalty payments to the publisher.[15] Before they enter the electronic services arena, libraries will therefore have to decide what kinds of costs they will charge back to their users. If they do not, they may find themselves subsidizing users or forced into frequent changes of policy, neither of which is a desirable end.

GUIDELINES

Because commercial document delivery is still very new, guidelines have not been developed. Moreover, the nature of electronic materials is still very much in flux. To a large extent, entities such as the Copyright Clearance Center have been in control, and libraries have not yet been able to evaluate the balance between their rights and their responsibilities. Nevertheless, it seems clear that libraries using document delivery services have stepped into a new world with new rules, and they will have to develop their own policies to cope with that world.

Libraries must decide whether they will recover total or just out-of-pocket costs. Only too often libraries feel that they should bear at least part of the cost—that relating to library staff costs. While this may reflect to their public roles, it begs the question of whether they are responsible for all costs associated with special needs. The situation is somewhat different for colleges and uni-

---

Choosing Between Interlibrary Loan or Document Delivery Services

- Are such transactions initiated at the reference desk or should they be referred to the document delivery service librarian?

- Should there be a dialogue about the differential costs involved?

- Should the librarian provide all the forms needed?

- How will these transactions be nestled into the general records of the document delivery service?

- How is delivery to be arranged?

- Who tracks the numbers of transactions involved?

versities, which already have a kind of compact with their users and may not feel able to charge for these services. The library is providing a special service, however, and the user could use other means to meet his or her needs. This argument may become less compelling as more and more information becomes available only in electronic format. Nevertheless, the fact remains that many users, particularly in the public library area, will not have personal access to electronic information and will have to rely on the library. Libraries will continue to face the issue of equal access, because it cannot be resolved by universal fiat and must be decided locally in accordance with the needs and abilities of the local community.

PAYMENTS

Both interlibrary loan and document delivery require decisions about the method of payment. Are credit cards, either personal or departmental, acceptable? What procedure is used for billing? Directly to the individual, to a departmental account, or to a corporate account? Who is authorized to initiate a charge? In some libraries, even individual reference librarians are encouraged to suggest to users that they should seek direct document delivery rather than interlibrary loan. The answers to these questions may well affect the general effectiveness of the service. The more staff members are involved, the more necessary it is to keep them all up to date with changes in the service—new vendors, charges, rules, procedures. Unless this is done, the library may find itself offering different versions of the same service.

Remote User Access

Many users will also want to take advantage of electronic communication, for example by sending in their requests from a remote terminal. Is there any procedure to determine whether the wanted item is actually held by the library, or will the library simply process any request received regardless of the end-cost to the user? If the goal is user satisfaction, it would be well to attend to such issues. The handling of remote requests will certainly be a factor in handling the results of distance education and, so far, there have been few general guidelines.[16] It seems likely that there will be more such studies and recommendations, and that the question

---

Figure 4.3 Checklist for Establishing Cost Recovery in Document Delivery

	Yes	No
Is there a basic transaction charge?	—	—
Does this cover all internal costs?	—	—
Or only nonpersonnel costs?	—	—
Is there a special fee for rush service?	—	—
Are all supplier charges passed on?	—	—
Service charges?	—	—
Photocopying charges?	—	—
Postal or other delivery charges?	—	—
Royalty charges?	—	—
Is there an account processing fee?	—	—
Separate?	—	—
Included in basic charge?	—	—
Can costs be charged to departmental accounts?	—	—
Are credit cards acceptable?	—	—
Personal?	—	—
Corporate?	—	—
Departmental?	—	—
Is there a standard billing period?	—	—
Is there a fee for late payment?	—	—

---

of interlibrary services will need to be addressed as well as the needs of the individual institution.

RECORDKEEPING

In both services, it is necessary to keep a record of success. Are supplier rates of fulfillment and speed of reply in line with their promises? If not, what remedial action is proposed? Studies have suggested that fulfillment rates do not always live up to the original promise.[17] Libraries are vulnerable to user dissatisfaction and should be prepared to monitor closely vendor performance. Are there areas where document delivery is not the best source of information? The alternative for international publications, or smaller publishers such as societies, may be the traditional interlibrary loan.

PUBLIC RELATIONS

It is essential that libraries clearly state all costs and charges. This is true for both interlibrary loan and document delivery. Individuals do not always understand that the general increases in costs caused by inflation or by new processes will affect their own transactions and may refuse to accept perfectly legitimate charges if they have not been informed in advance. The shift from traditional print-based activities to electronic information services represents a total change for libraries, which must now grapple with the costs of retrieving information that neither they nor other libraries "own." Moreover, many users will be even better versed in electronic access than many librarians (a situation often paralleled in schools where the students are better able to use their computers than are the teachers) and will consequently be prepared to challenge what they perceive as unfair charges.

If libraries do not consider these problems they may find themselves without a clear role in the electronic information age. Users need to know what access to information will cost them; the library's parent institution needs to know what costs are involved in providing library services and what kinds of costs will be recovered from users. Without this information it is impossible to set up appropriate budgets to support the needed services. Ultimately, the library's "image," as well as the efficiency and quality of its services, will factor into policymaking and fee collections. The New Zealand study that has been cited previously supports this paradigm, but cannot provide adequate leadership for libraries in other countries where both the economic and legal situations differ.[18] Nevertheless it demonstrates that there is an urgent need for such guidelines.

NOTES

1. Barbra Buckner Higginbotham and Sally Bowdoin, *Access Versus Assets: A Comprehensive Guide to Resource Sharing for Academic Libraries* (Chicago: American Library Association, 1993).

2. E-mail references to such problems are frequent, for example, Ruth Brown on coping with the high cost of copyright fees on journals, and responses from other librarians, which indicated the possibility of minimal copyright fees of $200.00 for articles from one journal, starting at $50.00 per article.

3. There have been numerous cost studies dating from the early 1970s, the most recent being that conducted by RLG (fully cited in note number four). Readers should be aware that conclusions drawn from the study of members of the Association of Research Libraries may not always be applicable to their own institutions. There are few other studies, but many individual libraries can provide relevant data.

4. Marilyn M. Roche, *ARL/RLG Interlibrary Loan Cost Study* (Washington, D. C.: Association of Research Libraries, 1993).

5. Mary E. Jackson, "Library to Library: To Charge or Not to Charge?" *Wilson Library Bulletin* 67 (June 1993): 94–95+.

6. Interloan in New Zealand is an agreement between participating libraries and was based on the idea that borrowing and lending by any one library should balance out. Several relevant documents are available from the New Zealand Library and Information Association. The latest policy document from the Joint Standing Committee on Interloan provides that "libraries will operate in a charged system with each library free to set its own charges, including a zero charge." Para. 5.1 These charges are controlled by the Copyright Act 1994, Sec. 51 (2) (b), and Sec. 52 (2) (c).

7. Jackson, p. 95.

8. William L. Whitson, "The Way I See It: Fee, Free, or Subsidy? The Future Role of Libraries," *College & Research Library News* 55, no. 7 (July–August, 1994): 426–427.

9. Higginbotham and Bowdoin, op. cit.

10. For instance Wright State, Cleveland State, and Wesleyan University libraries have circulated changes to their lending policies that included fees for photocopying and for each loan. These are only a few instances of the many changes that have taken place over the last few years.

11. Among such guides are: Roxann Butos, comp., *Interlibrary Loan in College Libraries* (Chicago: ACRL, 1993. Clip Note #16); Virginia Boucher, *Interlibrary Loan Practices Handbook*, 2nd ed. (Chicago: ALA, 1996); Leslie R. Morris, *Inter-Library Loan Policies Directory*, 5th ed. (New York: Neal-Schuman Publishers, Inc., 1995). Remember, however, that all such publications become outdated quite quickly.

12. Wayne Pederson and David Gregory, "Interlibrary Loan and Commercial Document Supply: Finding the Right Fit," *Journal of Academic Librarianship* 20, no. 5/6 (November 1994): 262–272; Kathleen Kurosman and Barbara Ammerman Durniak, "Document Delivery: A Comparison of Commercial Document Suppliers and Interlibrary Loan Services," *College & Research Libraries* 55, no. 2 (March 1994): 129–139.

13. Susan B. Ardis and Karen S. Croneis, "Document Delivery, Cost Containment and Serial Ownership," *College & Research Library News* 48 (November 1987): 624–27.

14. *Intellectual Property and the National Information Infrastructure: The Report of the Working Group on Intellectual Property Rights*. Chair Bruce A. Lehman (Washington, D.C.: Department of Commerce, 1995).

15. Sue Kennedy, "The Role of Document Delivery Services in Interlibrary Loan," in *Research Access through New Technology*, ed. Mary E. Jackson (New York: AMS Press, 1989), 68–81.

16. Association of College and Research Libraries. Standards and Accreditation Committee, *Guidelines for Extended-campus Library Services*. College & Research Library News 50, no. 5 (1989): 404.

17. Barbara Quint, "Connect Time: Where's Your Parachute?" *Wilson Library Bulletin* 66 (April 1992): 85–86.

18. Coopers & Lybrand, *Valuing the Economic Costs and Benefits of Libraries* (Wellington: New Zealand Library and Information Association, 1996).

Chapter 5

Reference Service Considerations

Until the 1970s virtually no consideration was given to charging for reference services. In general, library costs could be determined and included in a budget without determining if there was any derived income. The provision of reference services was simply another budget item, mostly under the category of staffing, rather than an expense element. The arrival of program budgeting and the increasing need to justify budget requests has changed that rather simple scenario. Reference budgets now include not only library materials of the traditional kind, staff, and staff support costs, but also elaborate and expensive electronic services. Reference services in the libraries of the 1990s are quantitatively different from those of the past. So many new access possibilities and alternative responses are available that the older model of one-on-one interaction based on readily available printed sources has become outdated. The funding of these services is, and increasingly will be, an important concern for library managers.[1] In order to provide the services asked for by users, libraries, faced with rising costs and relatively static budgets, may be forced to consider other possible sources of income, such as direct charges to users.

Technology, increased information resources, growing service demands, and dwindling budgets force libraries to rethink their stand and to consider the possibility of collecting fees. There are at least two reasons to consider fees: (1) to help pay for the service, and (2) to limit wasteful or over-use of a service. Unfortunately, there are few guidelines to help an administrator in making these decisions. The issues are complex, and there are large variations in how libraries deal with them. A 1993 study by the Urban Libraries Council found that while libraries might charge fees, there was no consistent rationale for those charges.[2] The decisions for any particular library will be based on that library's mission, staffing, funding, and the information needs of its user community. Service choices may be contingent upon cost rather than on providing access to information: a library may decide that it can offer a specific service only if it can recover some or all of the costs involved and must therefore decide whether or not to offer the service at all. When a fee for service is involved there may also be legal considerations. For example, the Washington state attorney general determined that the Seattle Public Library's plan to charge fees for new electronic services would be illegal because these were essential services.[3] As more and more reference material becomes available electronically, cost and legal issues will become increasingly important and complicated.

There are, however, some considerations that can be helpful in the decision-making process. A reference department should develop a policy statement that defines the population served and outlines what services are provided. Most libraries make a distinction between essential and extraordinary reference services, but this may be somewhat problematic. What one library considers a normal reference function another may consider an extra service designed to meet a single user's need. Determining the difference goes back to the library's primary mission. While the mission may help in determining whether or not to charge, it is still necessary to know what it costs to provide the service. Before deciding on whether or not to impose a fee, the reference department should undertake a cost analysis and user survey. This may seem a daunting request, but unless the library has some idea of what its expenditures are, and should be, supporting, it will have difficulty in presenting a clear budget request.

Budget/User Survey

- What are the actual costs of providing such services?

- How many users are affected?

- Who wants what services?

- What proportions are there between different kinds of services?

Another need is to discover what user responses to policies and procedures are likely. Charging may be so unpopular that the library will lose needed public support. Alternatively, users may be willing to pay for what are perceived as value-added services. Libraries must also bear in mind that the price of purchasing and maintaining a machine to collect money and/or to pay for the salary of an individual to staff a service area may be more than the monies that can be recovered through fees. Before deciding whether or not to charge for a service, reference staff will want to answer several questions.

In any case, before instituting charges, reference departments must consider the type, amount, and payee of a fee for a certain service.

If a library decides to charge fees for reference services, the reference department will also have to decide what types of payment will be accepted, how they will be collected, where they will be collected, and how the collection points will be staffed or maintained, in much the same manner as commercial photocopy services provide staff or change machines to enable users to take advantage of their services. Libraries have implemented several kinds of charging mechanisms. Some charge on a transaction or search basis. Others have instituted a membership fee to help defray the cost of electronic access. The latter would include funds that an academic library may receive from a student technology or library fee.

Figure 5.1 Checklist of Considerations for Establishing Value-Added Reference Services

	Yes	No
Does the department have a written mission statement?	—	—
Is this an ordinary reference function?	—	—
Is this an extra reference function?	—	—
Can the cost of the service be determined?	—	—
Is it legal to charge for this service?	—	—
Is it cost-effective to charge for this service?	—	—
Can the user community support costs?	—	—
Can the service be offered without charge?	—	—

COMMERCIAL ONLINE SEARCHING

Fees became an important issue when online searching was introduced in the 1970s. Unlike the purchase of a reference book, the telecommunication, database, and citation charges for an online search had no precedent in library budgets.

Online Search Concerns

- Were they capital purchases or service charges?

- Were they similar to telephone costs or to specific user responses?

- How should they be folded into the library budget, or should they be recovered as being specific to an individual user?

Figure 5.2 Checklist for Setting Reference Department Fees

	Yes	No
What is the cost of the service?	—	—
What costs will be recovered?		
Out-of-pocket costs?	—	—
All costs?	—	—
Partial costs?	—	—
No costs?	—	—
Can a per transaction cost be determined?	—	—
What type of charge will you assess?		
Flat fee?	—	—
Variable fee?	—	—
Who will pay for this service?		
Faculty?	—	—
Graduate students?	—	—
Undergraduate students?	—	—
High school students?	—	—
General public?	—	—
Business users?	—	—
External (or nonresident) users?	—	—

There are still no easy answers because of the nature of the transaction involved. Online costs are based on usage and are different for each service and database. The library can neither predict nor control these charges, which are therefore difficult to include in a budget. As distinct from regular uses of the library's collection, each use of a database carries distinct costs. The cost of a search in a reference book is difficult to calculate, since it is included in the cost of acquiring the book in question, and is, in any case, less than the cost of the book because it involves the user's expenditure of his or her own time. Online searches, on the other hand, present readily available costs, either at the end of a session or on an itemized bill from the provider. The difference has enor-

Figure 5.3 Checklist of Decisions Related to Fee Collection

	Yes	No
What type of payment will be accepted?		
Cash?	—	—
Check?	—	—
Credit cards?	—	—
Debit cards?	—	—
Departmental accounts?	—	—
Personal accounts?	—	—
User billed?	—	—
How are charges determined?		
User honor system?	—	—
Machine attached to system?	—	—
Charges readily available online?	—	—
Where is payment collected?		
Reference department?	—	—
Centralized location (e.g., Circulation)?	—	—
At point of use (e.g., debit card system)?	—	—
Who maintains the collection point?		
Reference staff?	—	—
Student assistants?	—	—
Commercial vendor?	—	—

mous psychological impact. Reference to charges on a supplier's bill makes charging back easier and more attractive.

Level of Service

Although cost is a consideration, there are many instances in which an online search is the only method of retrieving the needed information or is clearly cost effective in terms of the staff or user time involved. Libraries have to decide whether online searching is the most productive way to provide service and then whether

---

Figure 5.4 Checklist for Determining Who Will Perform the Search

	Yes	No
Librarian?	—	—
Patron?	—	—
Will students be trained to perform their own searches?	—	—
Will batches of searches be distributed to students?	—	—
When will a search be performed?		
As an initial approach?	—	—
After all other resources have been exhausted?	—	—

---

to charge for that service. There are many ways in which libraries utilize online services. Some libraries do not use them at all. If they do, they usually require that searches be performed by a librarian who has received specialized training—the optimal use of databases requires that the user be up-to-date on database protocols, which are constantly changing. Some libraries do an online search only when the librarian has determined this to be the most efficient and cost effective method to answer a question. Many libraries will print out information that is available only online and maintain it for in-library use. Others, particularly academic and large research libraries, offer extensive online searches at a patron's request.

A distinction is frequently made between a ready reference online search initiated by a librarian and a search that produces a custom-made bibliography or a detailed company report for a library user. The ready reference search may be considered an extension of normal reference service and not be charged back to the user; an extensive or personalized search beyond ready reference may require a fee that covers the cost of the search, at least partially. Here the collection of a fee has been justified by budget limitations and by regarding this search as a service that benefits

---

Sample Online Charges

- Graduate students and faculty receive free searches or a specified number of free searches with charges for additional searches (academic libraries)

- Flat per search fee, with less expensive databases subsidizing more expensive ones

- First ten citations free, with charges for any additional citations

- Ten-ten rule, the library pays for ten citations, the user for the next ten, the library for the next ten, etc.

---

one person rather than the community at large. In a corporate or university setting, it is possible that there are units or programs with research funds that include money for such searches.

Budget Considerations

Few libraries have budgets that allow unlimited, free online searching. A recent survey of academic libraries indicated that, of those institutions offering access to external databases, fifty-five percent recover costs from students and fifty percent from faculty.[4] In most cases it appears that libraries subsidize an online search by charging back only the direct observable costs—connect time and citations. The indirect costs for staff time, training, and equipment are not generally fully recovered. As with other fees, there are almost as many charging possibilities as there are libraries.

In all cases, costs and charges should be carefully negotiated with the user. At the University of Memphis, for example, users make an appointment with a librarian to discuss their research needs before requesting a search. During the presearch interview, the user agrees to pay a certain amount for the search. Cost estimates are based on tables, prepared for each database, that provide detailed cost figures. For instance, a search lasting five minutes and retrieving fifty citations on database X will cost $38.42. The library guarantees that any additional cost will be paid by the library.

Figure 5.5 Checklist for Deciding When Searches Are Performed		
	Yes	No
Ready reference	—	—
Librarian initiates	—	—
Patron requests	—	—
Faculty	—	—
Graduate students	—	—
Undergraduate students	—	—
High School students	—	—
Business users	—	—
External users	—	—

END USER SERVICES

Since online searching has been available for more than twenty years, it is fairly well covered in the literature.[5] Online services are increasingly being supplemented, however, by other end user services that present their own unique challenges. These services include those that charge on a per search basis and those that charge a subscription fee; other charges, citation fees or royalties, may also be included.

In making decisions about charging back search costs, it is helpful to consider the types of service being offered. As with other financial decisions, these will reflect the library's mission and budget. In a public library, the librarian may perform the search and hand the results to the user. In an academic library, reference librarians may teach students to search online resources and provide the student with free searches after an instruction session. In this instance, the indirect costs are regarded as part of the general educational costs of the institution, rather than costs assessable to the individual student. As opposed to librarian-mediated online searching, end user services are designed to be used without extensive training. They may be used by either the library patron or by the librarian.

Figure 5.6 Checklist for Selecting an End User Commercial Search Service

	Yes	No
Which types of commercial services can the library offer?		
Online service with charges by the minute and citation?	—	—
Service that charges a per search fee?	—	—
Subscription-based service?	—	—
Can the library mix these types of services?	—	—
Can the library estimate the costs involved?	—	—
Can the library totally absorb the costs of the service?	—	—

Some services, such as OCLC's FirstSearch, charge a specific amount for each search. Libraries may purchase a number of searches and use them as necessary, and they can take advantage of special offers. One difficulty with a pre-search option lies in estimating the demand for the service and the numbers of searches to purchase; another is the final distribution of the free searches purchased.

Another type of end user service requires libraries to pay a monthly or annual subscription fee to a vendor. This is an option for some of OCLC's FirstSearch databases, as well as for databases offered by Information Access Corporation (IAC), EBSCO, and others. Purchase decisions will be based on anticipated use, since the per search cost for a subscription service decreases as use increases. While one search on a database with an annual cost of $1,200.00 will cost $1,200.00, 12,000 searches on the same database will cost only 10¢ per search, hence the need to investigate possible usage. Because the actual usage cannot be anticipated precisely, a per search cost will be difficult, if not impossible, to determine in advance. Libraries that have chosen to charge back search costs appear to have a flat fee, such as $1.00 for thirty minutes, or $3.00 per search. Many of the fees and charges collected are typically concerned with printing and similar products, and are discussed in chapter three.

Databases on CD-ROM are another option similar to the subscription-based databases. CD-ROMs may be a one-time purchase, such as the *Oxford English Dictionary*, or involve an ongoing cost in the form of a monthly or annual subscription fee. Again, it is difficult to determine a per search cost. Some vendors provide statistical reports that can be used to predict costs. Ann Nista, Karen Albert, and Beth Lewis have reported on a menuing software for tracking usage for the possible recovery of CD-ROM subscription, startup, and operating costs.[6] Copicard, Inc., of Dallas, Texas, has announced an interface to its card-reader system that would allow libraries to charge for computer usage rather than printing only. With this interface, a user inserts a debit card and the card-reader deducts a preset amount for every minute of computer use. Here again the issue of institutional and individual responsibilities surfaces. Who pays for what will continue to be a major topic of debate.

Libraries are experimenting with different services and mixes of electronic resources. A library may need to have available a variety of databases offered by a commercial online supplier, such as Dialog or FirstSearch, and purchase the most heavily used databases on CD-ROM or as a subscription. This may not be a sufficiently broad basis, and libraries will need to look at subscription-based online services. Smaller libraries may wish to participate in consortial acquisitions of databases, since increased usage will lower the cost of each specific search.

INTERNET CONSIDERATIONS

In the 1990s the Internet became an important information resource. Originally conceived as a network through which scientists and other academic researchers would communicate, it has exploded with an enormous array of resources. The information available is growing at an exponential rate. Gil Baldwin, Chief, Library Division, GPO Library Service Programs, states "we expect that nearly all of the information provided through the Federal Depository Library Program will be electronic by the end of fiscal year 1998."[7] American Library Association President Betty J. Turock has stated, "Our goal is to make sure that every American has access to information online at their schools, public, college, and university libraries."[8] This raises a number of questions.

Internet Access Concerns

- How will libraries deal with this emphasis on technology and how will access to the Internet affect libraries?

- How will libraries pay for continued access after initial grants covering the costs of connection expire?

- Can these costs be covered through the regular budget process?

Some of these issues are discussed by Murray S. Martin, who suggests that many libraries will have to seek some measure of cost recovery but should always be aware of any restraints on open access.[9] Balancing these interests will always be a major library concern.

Academic libraries were among the first to encounter the Internet, probably because their computer services unit provided access. The allocation of cost has still not been adequately dealt with in institutional budgeting, and a totally new approach may be necessary if some of the proposed changes in copyright law are eventually enacted. Increasingly, however, public libraries are becoming connected to the Internet. A study by Charles McClure, John Bertot, and Douglas Zweizig found that 20.9 percent of the public libraries studied had Internet connections by 1994, and 12.7 percent had public access terminals for patron use. In most of these libraries, the staff used the Internet for their own purposes (using electronic mail, Telnet, etc.) or to retrieve material, especially government information, for patrons.[10] These numbers have risen dramatically since that time. Each issue of *LJ Hotline* contains newsnotes of further initiatives, often at the state level and funded with public money. Librarians have found electronic conferences (Listservs) to be a valuable professional tool.

Most of the information resources on the Internet are available

Figure 5.7 Checklist of Internet Usage Fees		
	Yes	No
Using an Internet browser?	—	—
Printing?	—	—
Personal electronic mail?	—	—
Disk storage?	—	—
Dial access?	—	—

and accessible through Internet browsers, either text-based (Gopher, Lynx) or graphic (Netscape, Mosaic). In addition to using these browsers, users may want electronic mail, along with the ability to connect to other computers (Telnet), and transfer files (FTP). Each library will have to decide on the appropriateness of each Internet service for its user population. The types of Internet services provided are directly related to costs, in terms of both connectivity and staff training. Although the popular press makes Internet access seem as easy as having a computer and picking up the phone, connecting to the Internet is expensive and complicated, with annual cost estimates per library ranging from $1,000.00 to over $15,000.[11] (An important resource for public libraries is *Internet Costs and Cost Models for Public Libraries*, by Charles McClure, John Bertot, and John Beachboard.[12]) It is becoming increasingly common for public libraries offering such services to charge a fee for establishing a personal presence on the Internet and for such services as setting up FTP (file transfer protocol) capability. Such services are clearly personal, and an annual fee seems appropriate.

Academic libraries may rely on their computer centers for Internet services but should carefully consider the type of access provided in the library in order to ensure that library resources are not monopolized by students using electronic mail or other Internet facilities in the same way as student "hackers" have managed to use library OPAC terminals for doing their computer center homework. Colleges and universities are continually looking for money for Internet access. Because of the increased demand for dial-up services, some institutions are examining outsourcing dial access and charging students a monthly fee. At the 1996 Charleston Conference, the Chancellor of the University of Tennessee at Knoxville described a subsidized scheme for student access but cautioned that it had been necessary to levy charges on nonresidential students despite the appearance of unequal service.[13]

Each library will need to determine the types of Internet access to provide. Locating and viewing information through Internet browsers is the most logical first step, and libraries will want to examine whether or not they will charge for this access and, in some cases, whether they are legally able to do so. Some libraries have decided to charge on a per minute basis, both to control use and recover costs. In addition to providing basic access to Internet information resources, some libraries are experimenting with individual Internet accounts for electronic mail and other services. The Carroll County Public Library (Maryland) charges residents $50.00 per year (nonresidents $80.00 per year) for disk storage and personal accounts. Charges such as these may become more common as libraries personalize services and look for funding to provide extended services.

REFERENCE SERVICES TO OFF-CAMPUS PROGRAMS

Many colleges, universities, and commercial educational corporations are offering classes and degrees to students outside their geographic areas through extended campus programs. These kinds of programs are in addition to the already existing "mail order" degree-granting universities that have mostly relied on other institutions for library and information services. A student in California or Alaska may attend college in Florida or Texas without leaving home. Central Michigan University has offered extended programs throughout the United States, Canada, and overseas for many years. Some universities offer degrees through CompuServe or the Internet. Library services to off-campus programs are "those services offered in support of academic courses and programs which are available at sites removed from the main campus."[14] There is a good deal of variation in the amount and type of library support for off-campus programs. Some parent institutions provide virtually no library service to off-campus students, while others provide extensive support. An institution may assign a librarian, make a separate department, or even create a separate library to serve off-campus students.[15]

New Zealand has for many years conducted a correspondence school for isolated students and provided library support through the lending of books, originally through the Country Library Service; the same is true in Australia, where students can connect with teachers through the radio. The Open University in Great Britain is another example of extended service that relies on access to other library collections. Libraries so involved will need to consider whether they will levy charges for use of their resources. In a public library, where the off-campus student is a resident of its supporting community, this may be difficult. Academic libraries will have to consider whether such uses fall within community or state mandates and whether there will have to be a charge for library use. Some of these issues are explored in chapter two.

Barbara Pease and Colleen Power provide an overview of reference services for off-campus students and faculty members.[16] The service goals are the same for both on- and off-campus students, but the delivery method is quite different. Students frequently do not come to campus, and reference service is handled by telephone, fax, or computer. Because off-campus students communicate with the reference department in the above manners, a user fee is assessed if the institution does not have an 800 tele-

---

Providing Off-Campus Services

- Does the library have sufficient staff for the librarian to perform a CD-ROM or a manual search for an off-campus student?

- Does the library require the student to travel to campus for this service?

- What does the library do if an online search is required?

- Once a search is performed, how are the results sent to the student and who pays the costs incurred?

phone number or provide for electronic reference service. Off-campus users may not have access to some resources, such as CD-ROMs or various print indexes, available to those on campus. In this case, the parent institution will want to consider mediated searches and determine whether or not to charge a fee to the off-campus student.

An institution may decide to provide free online searches for off-campus students or to charge a fee if it does so for on-campus students, but there are other issues in seeking to make on- and off-campus instruction equitable. A useful overview of these issues is provided in *Libraries and Distance Learning.*[17]

Figure 5.8 Checklist of Reference Services for External Users

	Yes	No
What reference services will be provided?		
Online searching?	—	—
CD-ROM searching?	—	—
Classroom orientations?	—	—
Written guides?	—	—
Designated librarians?	—	—
Online catalog access?	—	—
On-site reference collection?	—	—
Toll-free reference help?	—	—
Will these services be provided by the parent institution?	—	—
Will the parent institution make arrangements for library service with a local public, community college, or academic library?	—	—
How will responses to reference questions be delivered to the off-campus student or faculty member?		
Which services can be free?		
For which services must fees be collected?		

Figure 5.9 Checklist of Fees for Off-campus Student Services

	Yes	No
Do you charge off-campus students and faculty for		
Reference services?	—	—
Long distance reference telephone calls?	—	—
Long distance catalog access?	—	—
Long distance database access?	—	—
Mediated searches?	—	—
CD-ROMs?	—	—
Online searches?	—	—
Manual searches?	—	—
Document delivery, either e-mail or fax?	—	—

It is helpful if as much material as possible—particularly catalogs, bibliographic databases, and articles in full text—is available through remote access. However, the expenses associated with the emphasis on computer technology are high and will have to be paid for. The library may need to take monies out of its budget, possibly to the detriment of other services to students, or pass on the charges to the students themselves. A mix of these two approaches appears to be the most likely resolution, but institutions need to recognize more clearly than they have in the past the role that libraries play in student education.

OTHER CONSIDERATIONS

This chapter has examined some of the reference services for which a fee may be assessed. Depending on its mission, staffing, budget, user community, and governance any library may consider and justify charging for any service, particularly if that service is beyond the library's immediate mission and means. Some academic libraries, for example, have decided to charge for genealogy research (or may not allow such materials to be supplied on interlibrary loan), while others charge for answering reference questions by mail, particularly when photocopying is involved. A library can conceivably charge for a range of reference services, and managers will want to examine the issue of fees before introducing a new service, even if the decision is not to charge for that service. The basic issue is that reference service is costly, and libraries need to devote their regular budgets to their primary clientele. Extra services, or services to outside users, may well be subject to fees.

NOTES

1. As an aside, it is interesting to note that charging for services has a long history. In the 1930s some libraries charged for using the dictionary for more than fifteen minutes. See Joan Fortune, "Budgeting," in *Online Searching: The Basics, Settings & Management,* ed. Joann H. Lee (Littleton, Colo.: Libraries Unlimited, 1984), 67.

2. "ULC Reports Most Members Without Fee-Charging Policies," *Library Journal* 118, (1 May 1993): 14–15.

3. "News in Brief," *American Libraries* 25, no. 4 (May 1993): 377. There was a similar report concerning the Milwaukee Public Library in *Library Journal,* 1 September 1989.

4. Mary Jo Lynch, "How Wired Are We? New Data on Library Technology," *College & Research Library News* 57, no. 2 (February 1996): 99.

5. See Ed Cortez and Robin Rice, "An Investigation into the Role of Public Libraries with Online Reference Services," *Public Library Quarterly* 14, no. 2/3 (1994): 7–27; Joann H. Lee, ed., *Online Searching: The Basics, Settings and Management* (Littleton, Colo.: Libraries Unlimited, 1984); and Mary Jo Lynch, *Financing Online Search Services in Publicly Supported Libraries: The Report of an ALA Survey* (Chicago: American Library Association, 1982).

6. Ann S. Nista, Karen M. Albert, and Beth M. Lewis, "Cost Recovery and Usage Tracking of CD-ROM Databases with Menuing Software," *Medical Reference Services Quarterly* 10, no. 4 (Winter 1991): 15–27.

7. Gil Baldwin, "The Federal Depository Library Program in Transition" (paper given to the Federal Documents Task Force, Government Documents Round Table, American Library Association Midwinter Meeting, San Antonio, Texas, January 20, 1996).

8. Linda K. Wallace, "Advocating Equity: ALA's New Campaign," *College & Research Libraries News* 57, no. 2 (February 1996): 78. This movement is evident in the many news reports of state, foundation, and library initiatives showing that funds are being provided for initial Internet connections. It is less clear where future operating funds will come from.

9. Murray S. Martin, "Money Matters: Cost of the Internet," *Technicalities* 15, no. 3 (March 1995): 1, 5.

10. Charles R. McClure, John C. Bertot, and Douglas L. Zweizig, *Public Libraries and the Internet: Study Results, Policy Issues, and Recommendations* (Washington, D. C.: U. S. National Commission on Libraries and Information Science, June 1994).

11. Information about services for access is available through Internet directories such as Yahoo, Excite, or Magellan, or *Providers of Commercial Internet Access Directory* (available through <http://www.celestin.com>), or in books about the Internet such as Ed Krol's *The Whole Internet: User's Guide & Catalog*, 2nd ed. (Sebastopol, Calif.: O'Reilly and Associates), and Brendan P. Kehoe's *Zen and the Art of the Internet: A Beginner's Guide* (Englewood Cliffs, N. J.: Prentice Hall, 1994).

12. Charles R. McClure, John C. Bertot, and John C. Beachboard, *Internet Costs and Cost Models for Public Libraries: Final Report* (Washington, D. C.: U. S. National Commission on Libraries and Information Science, June 1995).

13. William Snyder, "The Information Technology Imperative for Higher Education" (keynote address at the Charleston Conference, Nov. 7, 1996).

14. Association of College and Research Libraries. Standards and Accreditation Committee, "Guidelines for Extended-campus Library Services," *College & Research Library News* 50, no. 5 (1989): 404.

15. Sherrill Weaver and Harold Shaffer describe a program in which Indiana University, Bloomington (IUB) contracted for library services for a distance graduate program. In this case the local academic library (IUB) set up and staffed a sepa-

rate library center for the distance education students. See Sherrill L. Weaver and Harold A. Shaffer, "Contracting to Provide Library Service for a Distance Graduate Education Program," *Bottom Line* 8, no. 3 (1995): 20–27.

16. Barbara Pease and Colleen Power, "Reference Services for Off-Campus Students and Faculty," in *Reference Services Planning in the 90's,* ed. Gail Z. Eckwright and Lori M. Keenam (New York: Haworth Press, 1994), 43–62.

17. Carolyn A. Snyder and James Fox, ed., *Libraries and Distance Learning* (Greenwich, CT.: JAI Press, 1997).

Chapter 6

Cooperative Library Service Costs

Most libraries have found that they can no longer go it alone. The complexities of electronic information, local budget problems, continuously rising costs of materials, the need for continuous staff training, and the costs of local processing have forced a revision of local independence. In most cases, libraries have found it essential to use the services of library utilities (OCLC, etc.) and their mediators, the regional or state networks. As they have moved further into automation, libraries have had to deal with system and database vendors, many of whom now offer a broad spectrum of services, some of which are costly to use. This shift in library services has brought about a similar change in libraries themselves. It is no longer simply a question of funding an individual library, but of finding ways of fitting local funding into area, regional, and national networks. The result is a much more complex fiscal setting. The individual library has to respond to more than its local needs; it must consider the ways in which it can participate in shared services in order better to address those needs.

Although not at first sight closely related to the issue of library fees and charges, membership costs, travel expenses, and payment for training have become an important factor in the "Other Expenses" budget category.[1] The reverse fee nature of membership costs makes them a part of the budgeting process. Memberships may appear expensive, but they can reduce other internal costs and help the library to function more efficiently. It is less an issue of determining what fees to charge than of deciding what payments are appropriate and whether there are costs that should be passed on to users. Some cooperative costs can become user costs similar to those of interlibrary loan and document delivery, because they are outside the regular library budget. If the cooperative provides services the local library cannot provide, and there is a resulting charge, the local library may have to determine whether to pass on those costs, which would otherwise become a charge on the general budget even though they were incurred for personal benefit.

MEMBERSHIP CHARGES AND COSTS

Most memberships in groups and networks relate primarily to automation, but many also involve shared resources or expenses. Institutional memberships in library associations, such as the Association of Research Libraries, are often a vital part of the library's existence. Other memberships, for example participation in an automated cataloging network, are unavoidable, for very few libraries can afford the luxury of independent cataloging endeavors. In other cases, it may be more practical for individual librarians to take out memberships, though there is always the fact that membership usually includes journals and other publications that can help all library staff in their duties. The issue may well be whether library or individual membership in a regional or local association is more valuable than membership in a national association. Because active participation requires attendance at meetings and conferences, the question of how to pay for or share the costs of attending meetings will also arise. Libraries may provide some measure of reimbursement for staff members, mostly for travel to meetings, but sometimes for membership dues. The library must decide what procedure to follow, based on the benefits received.

Weighing benefits against costs is even more important where there are multiple memberships.

> ### Choosing among Memberships
>
> - Which are the most important to the library?
> - Which offer the greatest benefits?
> - Which "go with the territory," and are thus unavoidable?
> - What are the real, as against the nominal, costs?
> - Are the benefits staff-related, operational, or user-related?

Small membership fees with large benefits are acceptable; the reverse is not. Determining which is the case is not always simple. Sometimes membership in a local consortium, while expensive in itself, can provide large benefits to library users through access to and use of other collections. It is important to realize that even if the library is a major provider of shared services, those services obtained from other libraries, for example, in a field where the library does not collect extensively, may be crucial for some users and ultimately save the library money. What kinds of consortia are available? Many, such as the bibliographical utilities and their associated networks, have no true alternative. Others, such as local consortia or groups of similar libraries, may duplicate or overlap services. Consortia may provide access to decision-making groups whose conclusions may affect other library activities. In each case, the library must weigh the cost of participation against the real and potential benefits of being part of a group that may substantially affect future actions and costs.

At least part of all memberships go to pay for the staffing of a central office. There may also be charges for specific services, such as training sessions, or for processing. The nature of such charges was explored by Barbara Ketterer,[2] who found a great deal of variability. It is possible to have a kind of laundry list, so that libraries can choose what services they will pay for and receive, but there may be effects on the membership status. There are often also charges for specific activities, such as preparing overdues or providing equipment. The maintenance and upgrading of equipment is a major cost and is usually more economically provided by membership in a consortium or utility. These kinds of considerations are important in determining participation in any shared activity. While many "dues" may seem excessive and a waste of library money, obtaining the same services they offer can be even more expensive in the local market. This is particularly true for training, which must always be provided externally, and for the development of policies and procedures, where going it alone may well result in an inferior product. In a sense, membership fees are similar to paying for consultants and part-time staff. Moreover, a single library may have very little influence over a bibliographic utility or an automation vendor, while a consortium or group may be able to change priorities in services. This can be a very important consideration when dealing with a major service vendor. Weigh the benefits against the costs to determine the best way of obtaining them. Such an examination will help the library decide whether membership is profitable and can also be used in helping determine the membership charges—these are seldom set unilaterally and often fall into several categories.

Evaluating Membership Products

- Can they be replicated locally for the same or a lower cost?

- Could they be provided at all from local resources?

- Are there alternatives, such as attendance at regional or national conferences?

- Are there added advantages from shared participation?

Remember that participation in the decision-making activities of a vendor or a utility is the equivalent of consortial membership. The resultant benefits can relate directly to the cost of local services, and participation may be essential if the library's objectivities are to be met. Evidence of the importance of such participation is provided by the large numbers of such meetings that take place in conjunction with American Library Association conferences.

There are, of course, associated costs, such as attendance by the library staff, but this can be interpreted as continuing education *and* maintaining the library's priorities within system development. In other settings the benefits are more indirect, such as influencing new technology or helping set local, regional, or group policies. These benefits should not be downgraded, but it is clear that any library must draw a line on total expenditure on cooperative activities.

MUTUAL FEES AND CHARGES

Many consortia develop programs for the sharing of resources. For example, members may be exempted from paying charges for interlibrary loans from other member libraries. Such groups may also provide free membership cards (often with a limit on the total number for any one library) or agree to mutual collection access by each library's users. Generally, cooperating libraries are determined either by geographical proximity or by similar programs and needs. The first may bring together dissimilar, but possibly complementary, libraries; the second may link libraries from different geographic areas. Each has its own operational problems but ensures a certain kind of enrichment for the individual library. Overlap between possible consortial memberships must also be considered. Sometimes memberships are unavoidable because of arrangements within states or legal requirements; others are voluntary. Are there overlapping benefits? If so, which memberships are most useful to the library? Remember that there can be great benefits from membership in a specific group or consortium and that the associated costs may be minimal. Discussing problems with similar libraries can reveal solutions; dialog may not occur so readily within a larger, more diverse group. Are any memberships essential in providing services to users, for example borrowing privileges that can readily be used, distinct from occasional usage, or access to a specific collection that will aid a significant proportion of the library's users?

In many instances, the level of interlibrary use is equivalent, and the result is a balance between the participating libraries. Each library gives and receives services—the optimal level for consortial participation. When a group includes one or more major libraries

Figure 6.1 Checklist for Assessing Consortium Costs and Benefits

	Yes	No
Membership fee?	—	—
Specific fees for services?	—	—
Training?	—	—
Overdue notices?	—	—
Automation costs?	—	—
Cataloging and processing?	—	—
Other? (list)	—	—
Other costs?	—	—
Travel?	—	—
Communications?	—	—
Benefits		
Purchasing discounts?	—	—
Shared access?	—	—
Consortium user cards?	—	—
Policy development services?	—	—
Consulting services?	—	—
Automation services?	—	—
Processing services?	—	—

that inevitably provide more services than they receive, the issue is whether the benefit is greater than the cost. Here libraries often fall into the fallacy of thinking that each service is equal, whereas the reality is that some services, such as access to rare and special collections or the ease of using a smaller library, greatly outweigh the average benefit of access to general collections. By looking at the totality of uses a library can determine whether a few major services equal many routine ones, making participation valid.

Added conditions can make memberships proscriptive. This is often the case with the use of special collections or rare materials—controlled access, no photocopying or copying by the staff only, no note-taking except in pencil, and limits to the numbers of items that can be consulted at any one time.[3] Moreover, such materials must generally be read in the library and may not be borrowed. There may also be the need for a supporting letter from the sponsoring library. While such conditions do not constitute fees or charges, they control use and have an intangible price. Consortial members must weigh them as part of the cost of membership. In many consortia, use of other libraries is limited to access to the collections. Borrowing may be possible through interlibrary loan or with the use of a consortium card. The latter rule requires the sponsoring library to issue a card to potential users. Because the library guarantees the safe return of borrowed materials, it becomes responsible for the replacement of lost or damaged books. Given such conditions, the library may levy a charge for the card, particularly if it is one of a limited number allowed the library and must be returned after use. Where such an arrangement exists directly between two libraries, a common practice is for each library to purchase a limited number of user cards, which can then be issued, following proper procedures, to library patrons. The cost of a card is seldom passed on to the user and should be seen as part of an access budget, since it is a substitute for purchasing materials or instituting interlibrary loan or document delivery transactions. Other costs that can be associated with consortial activity, for example, the costs and fees for overdue, lost, or damaged materials, should be recovered from the user, and it may also be proper to charge for the use of a library card.

Many consortia, particularly regional groupings of public libraries, allow users from any participating library to borrow materials by simply using their own library cards. There may be an agreement that provides some reimbursement if the level of external use reaches a given threshold, say ten percent. This is sometimes handled at the state level, in recognition of the library's contribution to general library needs. It may also be funded by supplemental budget provisions, rather than by a direct subsidy based on use. This is often the case where a state has developed a system of regional or district library service, as in Pennsylvania, where certain libraries have been so designated and receive supporting funds. In any case, a participating library will need to keep accurate records of use by community and external users to support any claim for budget support.

INTERLIBRARY LOAN

Although most of the matters concerning interlibrary loan and fees were addressed in chapter four, it is appropriate briefly to consider bilateral or consortial arrangements. These are generally more important for academic libraries but can involve public and special libraries; the latter are more likely to be so involved if the group is supported by a state or similar entity. Any such agreements may abrogate or reduce the fees usually charged to external borrowers. The range can be from total remission to the waiver only of the base charge.

Because major libraries often belong to several consortia, determining the conditions governing any particular loan can become very complex. The effects of such agreements are touched upon by Alice Mancini, who points out that the University of Tennessee at Knoxville has more than one hundred reciprocal agreements.[4] The goal should be to reduce paperwork as much as possible. In the long run, feeless transactions are most suitable for groups of equal libraries. Where one or more members are likely always to be net lenders, either some cost recovery or a reimbursement mechanism is appropriate. If neither of these solutions is possible, the fee schedules of participating libraries should be harmonized, so that the accounts resulting from intergroup transactions do not become unmanageable. Accounting mechanisms, such as those provided by OCLC, will cover only those transactions undertaken within each utility's control, however. Whatever the case, each library should produce a clear statement covering consortial fees, both as a staff guide and as information for users. These guides should also make clear what, if any, alternatives are available.

SHARED ACCESS

In this chapter, the term "shared access" is used not to cover mutual borrowing but the shared ownership and use of material. Some consortia make arrangements for individual libraries to purchase expensive sets, which are then not duplicated by other member

Figure 6.2 Checklist for Evaluating Consortial Interlibrary Loan Fees

	Yes	No
Is the external user fee remitted?	—	—
Are postal/transmission costs remitted?	—	—
Are photocopy costs remitted?	—	—
Fully?	—	—
Partially?	—	—
Are there any limits on use?	—	—
Is there an agreement for net lender reimbursement?	—	—
How is the amount determined?	—	—
By whom?	—	—
Reimbursement from an external source?	—	—
Or, is it within the consortium?	—	—
Is there the alternative of user (debit) cards?	—	—
Is there a cost for such cards?	—	—

libraries. These purchases may be made from pooled funds or by the individual library. They are regarded as "common" purchases whose use by other library patrons is free of cost. There will be costs involved, for instance duplicating microfiche or making photocopies (such costs fall within the regular rules of use), but there will be no additional costs for access. Because this method of resource sharing is location dependent, it has fallen into disfavor, often being replaced by coordinated acquisition procedures.[5]

Joint acquisition of a costly database has become increasingly common; the consortium itself may purchase or lease the database for common use by member libraries, or one library may act as agent for a group of libraries. Generally speaking, such a contract minimizes the total cost, because it is possible to negotiate terms better than those for multiple purchases at a higher unit cost. In either case, there must be some agreement on sharing the cost of the initial purchase or lease and a method for assigning subsequent search expenditures. While neither of these may result in what is technically a fee, both fall into the category of special expenditures and require some mechanism for recovering the costs incurred through use. As purchaser, the consortium will be expected to pass on and recover costs incurred by individual libraries, who will, in turn, absorb or pass on those costs to individual users according to their own policies. Where one library is acting as agent, it will have to carry on the same activities. There may, however, be administrative costs, which may be part of the consortial membership or direct reimbursement to the agency library. These costs may be pro rata, based on use, or a simple percentage of the total. In some instances, for example a group purchase of the *Current Contents* database from ISI or the shared purchase of the U. S. Census tapes, each library may have to submit a common percentage of the purchase price. This expenditure is then offset by any cancellations of existing subscriptions. The library may elect to place recovered subscription costs in an access budget to subsidize future use, but it is likely that it will also be necessary to recover some or all of the costs associated with later use of the database—search fees, the cost of print-outs or downloading, and mailing expenses. The amount recovered will be determined by local policies. While complicated, it is far easier for a group of libraries to negotiate cheaper rates than for each library to do so separately.

Cost Recovery

It may be inappropriate to recover the cost of database access, since that was part of the initial purchase price, but the cost of the documents retrieved may well be recoverable since they represent an individual benefit. Cost recovery decisions will be determined by the institutional attitude towards library use. If all print-out or similar costs are recovered, these costs will be charged to the user. If the library has decided to set aside funds to cover certain kinds of use, e.g., by students fulfilling course requirements, they may be covered by a central fund or subsidized. The main issue is whether the library or institution has decided that it will provide unlimited information access or charge for external use.

COMMERCIAL OR QUASI-COMMERCIAL SERVICES

The variety of commercial or quasi-commercial service available has expanded greatly in recent years. These may include acquisition and processing services, overdue notices, use records, document delivery, and database access (to other library OPACs as well as to commercial databases). Each of these will have its own rules. Many libraries, faced with the need to cancel serial subscriptions, have turned to commercial suppliers for the recovery of needed documents. The wide range and differing nature of such services makes universal conditions the exception rather than the rule. Should such charges be passed on or absorbed by the library? There may be membership costs, e.g., USBE (Universal Serials and Book Exchange), or per transaction fees. In either case, the library must determine whether any of these costs should be passed on to the user. Membership costs appear to be the cost of doing business with a specific vendor and unrecoverable except within the context of fee-based or document delivery services, as discussed in chapter four. If the costs are simply a fee-per-use charge the library must determine whether to recover them.

Vendor Contracts

Many automated system vendors make it possible for participating libraries to gain access to databases, whether other libraries' OPACs or commercial products. The costs involved will be determined by the vendor's original agreement or by user libraries' negotiations. Again, the decision must be made whether to pass on transaction costs to the individual user. This would seem inequitable in the case of OPAC access, but reasonable in the case of using a commercial database. The promise of easy access has persuaded many libraries to substitute access for ownership. However, the switch may conceal many costs. It is likely that there will be royalty fees for recovered articles. There will also be administrative costs that the provider will not absorb. Libraries need to weigh the presumed benefits against the actual costs and determine whether or not to pass on those costs to users. Even minimal use of a service can result in substantial costs to the library.[6] To some extent, this merges with the decision as to whether the library will develop a document delivery service, often as a part of interlibrary loan, and where it will be located.

Other services are offered by many regional automation services, such as, the provision of overdue notices, special reports, and extended cataloging services. Commercial book suppliers like Baker & Taylor provide catalog cards, electronic records, or processing at an additional cost. Libraries need to look at these possibilities from two perspectives. Will using a central service reduce local work pressures? Is the service better than that provided locally? In particular, libraries should determine whether such aid will help them to improve service without levying added fees or charges on their users. If the answers to these questions are positive, the library should participate. These issues are especially relevant if the library is seeking to restructure internal services such as interlibrary loan or if there is great pressure on circulation to respond quickly to local need, without having also to cope with more mundane duties such as writing out overdue notices. There is, however, a need to consider any lapse of time in supplied services. The book may well have been returned before the notice reaches the delinquent patron. Delivery of articles by commercial services varies greatly, both by supplier and by subject area, as does the ability to provide the needed material.[7] The issues reach far beyond simple financial considerations, but they must always be taken into account when contemplating change. The general goal is to improve user access to information while deciding whether to recover the costs involved in meeting individual needs.

Can the library absorb costs or must it seek to recover its expenditures from the individual user? This question is also raised when providing Internet access: the library may decide that general access should be free but that the maintenance of a personal page or extensive printouts should incur a personal charge. Participation in a regional program can reduce expenses, but it may also reduce the kinds of access available. The initial costs are often supported by federal or state grants, but the ongoing costs tend to be charged back to the library, which must consider its own long-range needs and costs and determine whether it needs to pass on any consortial costs to its users. The latter decision will also require the harmonizing of internal and external costs so that the user will not feel frustrated in seeking information that is not immediately available locally.

NOTES

1. Sherman Hayes, "Budgeting for and Controlling the Cost of *Other* in Library Expenditure: The Distant Relative in the Budgeting Process," in *Financial Planning for Libraries*, ed. Murray S. Martin (New York: Haworth Press, 1983), 121–131.
2. Barbara A. Ketterer, "Library Automation Consortia: What Fees Should Members Pay?" *Bottom Line* 6, no. 2 (Summer/Fall 1992): 23–27.
3. Michael Carpenter, "How Can We Improve Resource Sharing? A Scholar's View," *Advances in Resource Sharing* 1 (1990): 58–73.
4. Alice Duhon Mancini, "Evaluating Commercial Document Suppliers: Improving Access to Current Journal Literature," *College & Research Libraries* 57, no. 2 (March 1996): 126.
5. Rodney Erickson, "*Choice* for Collection Development," *Library Acquisitions: Practice and Theory* 16, no. 1 (1992): 43–49.
6. Mancini, p.126.
7. Kathleen Kurosman and Barbara Ammerman Durniak, "Document Delivery: A Comparison of Commercial Document Suppliers and Interlibrary Loan Services," *College & Research Libraries* 55, no. 2 (March 1994): 129–139.

Chapter 7

Miscellaneous Considerations

There are many less obvious services that a library might provide for a fee, and such results should be considered in setting up a library budget. The possibilities range from the rental of equipment to providing coin-changers.

EQUIPMENT RENTALS

Years ago, before the advent of PCs, libraries, particularly academic ones, might offer rental typewriters by the hour for use in dedicated rooms. The charges were based on such factors as the life of the equipment, the need for servicing, and the replacement of ribbons. In one library known to the authors, students from a neighboring dormitory jimmied an emergency exit and made off with six typewriters. The students were caught and the typewriters recovered, but the library decided to discontinue so vulnerable a service. Nowadays, the parallel is renting out portable computers, more likely in a public than an academic library, because the latter's college may itself have made arrangements for renting computers.[1] As with typewriters, the fees charged will need to reflect amortization costs, maintenance and repair (including the upgrading of software), and the cost of handling accounts. There are no strict guides as to what libraries could charge; at best, they can make comparisons with commercial services and determine whether they want to match those charges.

System Time

Another alternative is to sell library patrons time on the local Internet access system, using one of the library's own computers. Here the questions about what to charge become more complex, because much will depend on what the computer is used for, which may vary from simple word processing to complex Internet searches. Responsibility for specific costs incurred is also an issue, since the computer is library owned. Many programs require the use of a password, but others can be accessed without any special requirements. There may be charges for access, downloading, printing, or entering messages. All such charges must be considered by a library setting up such an access system. The wisest solution is to require library patrons to use their own Internet (or similar) accounts just as if they were using a telephone charge card: the library simply has to decide what kind of general charge to levy. There are, as yet, few guidelines. Although some libraries provide the service free, the same caveats as attended free photocopying still apply, namely that the library cannot afford to supply free service to all users.

Any charge or fee should not be so low that it becomes a burden to handle the resulting cash flow and the related paperwork. The library will still need to service and upgrade the equipment. The latter is often overlooked, but it is clear from the voluminous literature on computers and electronic programs that yesterday's computers are already overdue for the trash heap. There are also specific kinds of services that libraries may want to provide, such as maintaining a personal account on one of the service providers, transferring files via the FTP (File Transfer Protocol) provisions, and even receiving and housing replies to personal e-mail. Some users may work from their own floppy disks, but others will want the library to provide storage. The advent of a new type of computer linked directly to the network presents another variation where the user product is stored centrally. In that case, the library or institution may well want to impose a carrying charge. These issues will greatly affect the ways in which libraries participate in the Internet.

All these matters carry costs, and the library should seek to recover whatever cash outlay is involved. In much the same way as local centers have developed for handling telefacsimile services, there will probably be computer service centers, and libraries will have to consider whether they are competing with them or are providing a community service, especially to the poor and disadvantaged. Because this kind of service is still in its infancy, many more issues will undoubtedly arise. Even the latest announcement from Washington that the government does not intend to impose any new taxes on commercial transactions via the Internet is only a brief respite. The barrier to such uniform taxes relates to the location of the user and the location of the respondent, each of whom may be subject to different state or national law codes. Libraries should perhaps make any users aware that shopping via the Internet is not permitted or that they must assume personal responsibility for any taxes incurred (hence the desirability of having users set up their own personal websites).

Operational Costs

Although many states and other authorities have provided school and public libraries with the hardware and software necessary for their initial access to the Internet, there has been much less financial support for ongoing operational costs. Once these systems are in place, library users will seek benefits from them. Libraries will want to respond to these needs but will also have to consider whether they can support such access without charge. Without any clear directives on how they are to respond to these legitimate requests, libraries will be left to determine individually their own guidelines. The result could be the same kind of chaos that surrounds overdue fines or interlibrary loan charges. One can only imagine the complex directories that might result!

ELECTRONIC NETWORKING

New as it is to libraries, the electronic network is an enduring fact, and libraries will have to develop policies to deal with its use. It is virtually impossible to provide uniform guidelines, however, because there are almost no measuring points. The cost of any service depends on its nature, its length, and whether it also involves charges from other parties. Hidden at present is the basic cost of travel over the network, because those costs have been absorbed by government agencies. At some time this will change, because the United States government, essentially the first sponsor of the Internet, has determined that the latter's future growth must be supported by private investment. If all users must eventually pay their way, then many institutions will have to reconsider whether they can freely provide access to all patrons. In these circumstances, the best advice to libraries is to keep up with all changes on the Internet. This may not be easy and requires attention to a wide range of protocols, service agreements, and changes in software and hardware.

FROM THE SUBLIME TO THE RIDICULOUS

Whereas handling the problems of the electronic world has the overtones of science fiction, the day-to-day difficulties of handling the needs of library patrons will often seem mundane and too ridiculous to need attention. Oddly enough, one of the perennial problems in libraries has been the need to provide pencils for the taking of brief notes, for example call numbers from the catalog. Only too often, these pencil stubs have been stolen, leaving later users without an essential service. Without access to pencils, borrowers have been known to tear out catalog cards. Libraries would not necessarily discover this for some time, and the perpetrators would long since have vanished.

That specific situation no longer pertains with online catalogs, but the need to record and transfer information does. There is no direct substitute for the pencil, but most libraries provide print-out facilities so that users can download the information they need. This falsely seems costless to the institution: setting up printers, providing paper, toner, and the like is much the same as providing photocopy facilities, but libraries have generally regarded this as inherent in their business. In most instances, it would probably be judged a basic service for which the library cannot charge, but that might not be the case with long-distance access, which also ties up a telephone line. There is little guidance available so far, although independent information providers include such costs in their hourly rates and may also detail specific costs incurred. In the few instances when public libraries have decided to charge for telephone or online reference services, the judicial responses have been contradictory: permitted, for example, in San Francisco, but not in Seattle. The same is likely to be true of online catalog consultation.

Online Files

There is a wide range of online services that can be provided. Many libraries have already decided that they have to charge for setting up personal accounts. The library, after all, has to monitor usage, provide adequate file protection, and maintain the appropriate records. There are also vendor charges to be considered. Even the charges of $60–80.00 a year imposed by some libraries do not seem to meet costs or address any issues of responsibility. While such services may be deemed to be in the public interest, there is also the question of whether they can or should be paid for or subsidized with public funds. Libraries may well find that they have to institute charges to prevent the abuse of library services without any reimbursement.

Personal Lockers

Lockers have been considered necessary because libraries needed to guard their collections against theft (although there are now alarm systems connected with the barcoding of books that can prevent at least some kinds of theft), and to protect the possessions of their users. Of course, it was virtually impossible to provide as much storage as was needed and was difficult to handle the kinds of equipment any user might bring into the library, such as a knife, without a body search. We might consider the changes in airport security; they may seem unrelated, but libraries have to face the fact that they are equally vulnerable to theft and mutilation of their holdings. On the other hand, there is little point in requiring users to deposit their belongings in lockers or similar storage places if there are many ways of avoiding being caught for theft. Libraries have long since given up on persuading their users to exercise the appropriate caution over what they bring to the library. Now that laptops and similar electronic equipment are common, libraries can only hope that their users will exercise more common sense. Some people find this kind of security for belongings they will not need for their work in the library a useful service, however. Many libraries, such as the Library of Congress, provide the service without charge. Others realize that there are associated costs and that they need to be reimbursed. As with typewriters and so on, this is a totally personal service and, as such, should be subject to a charge. There may be complaints that the fee results from library policies and should be a library responsibility, but the response is that the policies are clearly stated and conformity with them is a personal responsibility. The amounts of the charges levied is a matter of the marketplace, with charges being made in other public facilities providing a guide. Coin-operated lockers are certainly preferable to having the library staff handle other people's belongings.

Change Machines

One of the most difficult problems faced by any library is the making of change, whether after the payment of a fine or for use in one of the many machines now common. This involves a great deal of staff time, leaves loose cash around the library, and requires daily record keeping. In high risk areas many libraries require that their employees not bring any cash or valuable item into the library proper, leaving them instead in personal lockers. While this reduces personal risks to the employees, it does not solve the problem of keeping a till for making change for library users. Many libraries have installed change machines. Such machines are also frequently provided by photocopy services. It is best if these machines are maintained by an outside vendor, though the nature of the contract may require the presence of library personnel when the machines are being emptied, for example when the library receives a proportion of the total profit. Even so, this is better than tying up staff time handling cash. Similarly, if there is a refreshment area or cafeteria in the library, this should be run as a separate enterprise and include the provision of its own change machines. The increasing use of charge cards, including personal accounts at an institution, has reduced this problem to some extent, but most cards have handling charges that make them unsuitable for very small amounts. Personal accounts may differ, and there are frequently departmental accounts for miscellaneous expenditures. The most difficult issue is making sure that the account is genuine or that the charge is permitted.

Circulation Charges

The only situation where it is impossible to avoid handling cash is the circulation desk, where users will seldom have the exact amount for paying fines or rental fees. Because each transaction concerns small sums of money, the accounting problem tends to be overlooked. As the Scots say, "Many a mickle makes a muckle." Over even one day the total handled can become quite large, and the accounts horrendously complicated. Moreover, receipts should be given to maintain a public record. Libraries tend to record only daily totals, but this is little help when a particular payment or charge is challenged. Automated accounting can help with the record keeping, but requires extra staff time to set up and maintain. Libraries must decide what staff costs are recoverable and what are general administrative costs.

One goal should be to reduce to a minimum the places in the library where cash is handled. Although it may seem a service to the user to make it possible to conduct his or her transactions anywhere within the library, it is highly desirable to centralize the handling of cash for much the same reasons as for centralizing printouts. Major reasons for this are that: first, it enables the library to keep better records; second, it reduces the numbers of staff involved; and third, it discourages frivolous uses.

If there are many departmental (as in a university) or a number of business accounts, central record keeping is advantageous. This record, however, is separate from the accounts that must be kept by any fee-based service, such as document delivery, or any service operated by an outside vendor. It might even be advantageous to consolidate these activities with the library's accounting office, but feasibility would depend on ease of public access and the ability of the central staff to handle the extra business. Apart from these rather more elevated concerns, handling cash requires the provision of such items as cashboxes, cash registers, and record books or software. There will also be a need for safe overnight storage facilities, since most library central offices close long before the library itself. All these issues require that libraries carefully consider their ways of handling cash and assigning receipts and payments to the proper accounts.

BOOK SALES

Although the general objective of book sales is to generate income for the library, there are many factors that need to be considered. The first, IRS-related, issue is whether the proceeds are subject to income tax. This may seem remote from most libraries' settings but can become important if there are questions about the methods of evaluation and any statements provided to donors. There are also financial considerations. For instance, most librarians are probably unaware that books provided for review are income to the reviewer, who cannot then claim their cost as an income tax deduction if they are subsequently given to a library. The library should therefore not provide the "donor" with a record suggesting that the total value is tax-deductible. Donations of books and periodicals will mostly contain materials unneeded by the library, and donors should always be informed that donations will be disposed of in accordance with the best interests of the library. There may be difficulties in disposing of unneeded materials and substantial costs involved in sending them to other locations, though such institutions as the Universal Serials and Book Exchange can provide an appropriate outlet. It is no longer a matter of recognizing donors but of placing the library within an appropriate network of donations and purchases.

There are therefore two sides to the problem. The first is the adequate evaluation of donated materials, which may require that the library hire experts in the field. Establishing their value may cost almost as much as the return on their sale to rare book or second hand dealers but is preferable to arbitrarily pricing, and thus devaluing, an item. The second is in determining appropriate selling prices. Although it may be easier simply to set block prices for hardback and paperback publications, there will always be some items that have a different and others that have virtually no market value. Issues of the *National Geographic* magazine are in the latter category, because there are so many personal copies. Libraries therefore will have to determine individual and categorical costs for items being sold. These kinds of sales are best staffed by Friends or similar groups, but the library is in the best position to supply the evaluation expertise. There are many sources for the needed information, but it may not be easy to consult them within the time limits imposed by a library book sale. Basically, the same rules apply as those dealing with lost books. The library can decide either to look for specific sale prices per book or adopt categorical prices. A preview of what is being offered can be used to remove rare or valuable items that can then be sold for higher prices. But, again, it is important that such sales be under the aegis of Friends or similar groups, who transfer the profits to the library as a donation. This may appear complicated, but is an important factor in preserving the library's nonprofit status.

LIBRARY SHOPS

The same rules that apply to book sales apply to shops that sell publications or other library-related materials. Sales of this kind will vary in their economic impact depending on their relation to regular library activities. Some libraries have established a tradition whereby they generate substantial revenues. While their objective is to generate library income, such shops must distance themselves from the library itself. If they do not, they may jeopardize the library's nonprofit status. They should be operated by Friends groups or similar organizations, and their accounts should be totally separate from those of the library as a separate fund-raising activity. There are few, if any, guidelines on what libraries should demand of their ancillary organizations. The most important appears to be the need to maintain a distance from the library so that any income can be considered unrelated.

PUBLICATIONS

Many libraries attempt to increase both their income and their support group by providing publications for sale. Again, it is highly desirable to handle such activities through a Friends group rather than have the library handle a commercial transaction. These publications may range from Christmas cards to substantial monographs, but each must either have a sure sales volume or support from friends. Bookmarks and similar smaller items may be relatively easy to handle, but more substantial publications require a greater investment and a more assured market.

NOTE

1. A good example is the University of Tennessee at Knoxville, where resident students are supplied with computers and access to the Internet (nonresident students receive a subsidy instead), as described by William Snyder in his Keynote Address, "The Information Technology Imperative for Higher Education," delivered at the 1996 Charleston Conference.

Chapter 8

Overview of the Issues

While it may often appear that the library should be able to offer free service to all users, this general rule may not apply to all services or to all users. The earliest library/user circulation relationship was based on a one-to-one ratio—the user borrowed a single book at a time—and each transaction was singular in nature, since the resulting records applied to one book and one person, even if the latter borrowed several books at the same time. As libraries expanded and included reference services, business was still usually handled one-on-one, between one librarian and one client, even though there might be several questions in a specific reference session. Given these constraints, these services were fairly standard and could be assigned to costs that lay neatly within the general library budget. As the definition of information diversified it became possible and necessary to isolate specific needs and assign them to specific library programs, raising the issue of whether some services should be subject to a fee or other charge. This movement towards the separation of services includes interlibrary loan, the various media, and the whole range of electronic services, including access to databases or to online information, neither of which is within the library's financial control, and which, therefore, differ from the purchased resources that were the basis of earlier transactions.

Unfortunately, the specifications required changed the definitions of client and provider to the degree that it is now very difficult to determine clearly who is asking for information and who is providing it (the Internet and similar providers do not make clear distinctions). The complexities of the Internet and of information delivery sytems make elaborate reading of access protocols an essential part of service and charging. Because an infinite number of information creators (who have in the past been publishers), intermediaries (e.g, vendors), and information providers (e.g., libraries) all participate in the process of delivery, it is infinitely difficult to identify precisely each group's hand in costs and charges. In due course this problem will be solved, but it will undoubtedly take some time, given the compexities of copyright and contract law involved. Because libraries function as the final intermediaries in this process (the transfer of information from the provider to the user), their role is even less clear. Should they recover any secondary charge, or are they supposed to recover only the costs associated with photocopying or downloading, the equivalents of what they charged for in the paper age?[1] These issues are unlikely to go away, regardless of whether librarians wish to provide free service, because that service competes with other, commercial services and needs to prove its worth in the marketplace.

Libraries must consider what kinds of needs they are best situated to provide, and what kinds need external assistance. Because we no longer necessarily rely on a printed book for the retrieval of information, we have moved into a totally new information universe.[2] The flurry of competing electronic service providers, together with the emergence of a new generation of information seekers (brought up with the Internet), ensures that libraries will have to rethink their role and decide what they will or will not have to charge for information access. It is no longer simply a question of determining whether a specific book or article exists, but of whether the relevant information may also exist in an electronic version and, if so, if it is possible to retrieve it readily and how it might be reconfigured to be more useful. These processes are indeed different and involve separate allocations of cost. Formerly, libraries could view their budgets as paying for people, materials, and support costs; now all three intermingle in the provision of any service to the user.[3] This point was made repeatedly at the 1996 Charleston Conference, where several speakers referred to budgets as fluid rather than static. Change is now constant and needs to be reflected in the ways librarians think about fees and charges. The immense extension of the information available makes it even less likely that the library will be able to maintain a local collection that matches its users' needs. Closing the gap calls for ingenuity and new budget concepts. The "access" or "resource" budget has become a common idea but has so far done little except replace the "library materials" budget or expand it to include electronic resources.[4] It has not grappled with the need to proceed much more directly to program or performance budgets where all the elements supporting each transaction are taken into account.

Most librarians are used to dealing with an information universe where there are clear distinctions between providers, mediators, and users. Here the problem is less the kinds of media involved than the ways of making them work together. If library users were to be able to use properly all kinds of media, they needed to have equal access to all. This was a relatively straightforward viewpoint in the pre-electronic age, and it must now be adjusted to cope with changes in the delivery mechanisms for information. All media have inherent costs. Some, for example books, represent a one-time cost to the library. Others, for example databases or electronic publications, carry annual and/or use charges that the library may not be able to absorb. How these differing cost bases should be reconciled in the interests of equal access to information presents libraries with significant policy decisions. Some of these issues were discussed by Diane Tebbetts, who examined the real cost of library services.[5] Policy is the basis for all financial decisions, though the reverse often seems to be the case.

To provide equal access to information, libraries need to arrange for all their users to be able to access the kinds of information resources available to others. In the electronic era, this goal is less easily attainable than in a time when printed materials were the standard. It is also more difficult to define. Whenever there are direct costs associated with the retrieval of information for an individual user, libraries have to consider whether they should be absorbed or passed on to that user. Failure to consider any indirect costs may complicate the library's budget plans and make it difficult to arrive at an appropriate assignment of costs. Service institutions are often caught up in this kind of problem, because they are less concerned with their own costs than with their users' needs. They must, however, consider whether they can continue to meet those needs without either public or user funding. The accumulation of individual costs can make it impossible to support general needs.

SERVICE CHARACTERISTICS

In determining what kinds of charges to pass on to users, libraries will have to differentiate between basic and value-added services added. It may be difficult to determine which is which, but it is likely that any service where the library has to provide special assistance, set up added service points, or add special equipment may be considered to provide added value. For public libraries, this may be controlled by statute or, at least, by legal interpretation of those laws. Legal interpretations may reverse earlier decisions, but the resulting litigation can delay actual decisions for years. Academic libraries need to obtain administrative or, possibly, academic senate approval. Special libraries will need to show exactly how these charges harmonize with the mission of their institutions and how they can be recovered, if at all. Libraries will also need to differentiate between kinds of user in relation to services required. This is a basic consideration in the New Zealand experiment referred to earlier.[6] Even though the costs of each service may be equal, the local community provides basic financial support for general services to its members but not necessarily for special services to local or outside users. In either setting, the library or user must be aware of what costs are absorbed, what are reimbursed, and what must be recovered. The library budget is an investment in information retrieval, and the town or college budget is based on providing needed services to participants, including library services. Each participant will have a differing interpretation of what is necessary and what should be paid for. Reconciling these perceptions is not easy, but the task has become an inescapable fact of modern librarianship.

Academic libraries face the same problems as public libraries, but with a slightly different cast. The community in question is enclosed and self-defined—students, staff, and faculty. All have a specific stake in the institution's success, albeit in somewhat different manners. The academic library is therefore less able to impose charges for services that are expected as part of the community's educational goals. This attitude may be changing as more and more institutions charge technology and library-related fees, but this does not vitiate the basic premise that library services are part of the student-university agreement, though there may be specific services that carry an additional cost. Only too often, academic administrations have behaved as if the introduction of new information technology would solve all the financial problems of library support. They have not yet realized that the new information requires the same kind of intermediation as did printed information and providing this service may be even more expensive. Librarians need to make this point as clearly and as often as necessary, even while they may be seeking special rates on the Internet due to their public role. Unless this point is understood, libraries may find themselves unable to participate fully in the electronic age, to everyone's loss. Access to information is part of the compact surrounding copyright, though frequently the issue is who pays for access. If the library has paid for a determined number of accesses, or has paid for online access, it may be necessary to determine what costs the library or the individual user should pay.

Library Response Capacity

Problems arise when user needs venture beyond the basic capacity of the library. These issues are not confined to the ability to purchase wanted materials; they include the need to consult information available only in electronic format. In providing services, the library must carefully consider its responsibilities (and limits) to its patrons.

> ## Determining the Library's Responsibilities
>
> - If it cannot purchase and provide most of the materials needed free-of-charge, whose responsibility is it to provide what else is required?
>
> - Should there be added charges or should the institution pay for an individual user's needs?
>
> - What combination of free and charged services is acceptable?
>
> - Are there limits to the kinds of service the library should provide?

As soon as such questions are asked, the issue of fees and charges will come up. Libraries need to be prepared to respond with realistic policies. There must be some allowance for users who are economically disadvantaged or who have special needs (e.g., the physically handicapped) so that their information needs continue to be met. Care has to be taken to avoid the appearance of charity or any other stand that might be taken as offensive, but the notion of equalization seems to avoid this problem. There should be no question that special services to the visually handicapped, for example, carry no extra charge, even though the library may have to expend considerable sums of money to provide equipment or specially printed works. Vendors have to be sensitive to these kinds of needs. The differences between visually and auditorally handicapped library users and the general user of the library require the library to provide adequate services without charge-back costs.

CATEGORIES OF FEES AND CHARGES

As was suggested in chapter one, there are several reasons for imposing fees or charges. The clearest category is the compliance fee, for instance fines for keeping library materials beyond a due date. There are unlikely to be any legal objections, since it is clearly intended to make library materials more readily available. The same argument can be applied to charges for rental copies of highly popular materials, since the alternative would be long reserve lines or the expenditure of larger sums of money on evanescent materials. Charges for placing a reserve or for failing to heed a recall notice are similarly oriented, and most librarians will be able to think of other settings where the fee or fine is intended to enforce compliance with library policy. Less straightforward is the issue surrounding the claim that a service is for individual rather than community benefit. In the past, libraries have usually provided all services without thinking whether they served only one individual or not. With the advent of electronic services, costs have risen substantially, and the issue of charging has become important. Interlibrary loan and document delivery provide excellent examples. Although both are efforts to repair local failure, they may carry differential benefits and costs. Borrowing a book, which will then be returned to the owning library, seems simply an extension of the library itself. Buying an article or other publication for the use of one person is an individuated service for which a charge is suitable, especially because the other providers in the chain are certain to make their own claims for reimbursement.

Providing electronic reference information or the resulting materials presents another conundrum. Although in the past libraries have simply seen reference questions as a direct public service designed to forward the library's and the institution's mission, this was possible only because they did not usually involve significant actual costs. The indirect cost of providing the reference staff was viewed as required in order to make the library's collections accessible. Now that there may be substantial added costs, this position has to be reconsidered. If there is an alternative, say the use of printed reference works, the added value of electronic service may well be recovered; if there is not, the library will have to consider some kind of subsidy. This may be a matter of recovering only the out-of-pocket costs involved or of providing a certain number of free searches to the user. Full cost recovery may be considered in the case of external users, and it may even be necessary to deny service where there is no possibility of recovering the costs, as with casual international contacts via the Internet. Consortial and other agreements about shared services may affect these decisions. Because it is more difficult for the staff to cope with an ever wider list of who gets what and what kinds of exceptions are to be made, libraries should be wary of becoming involved in too many such groupings. Resource sharing agreements are beneficial but can become too complex to administer adequately.[7]

HANDLING FEES AND CHARGES

Each decision to impose a fee or other charge (including fines) carries with it the need to provide a mechanism to collect the monies involved. The method chosen should be the simplest possible, even if it may require the library to set up credit card accounts. The handling of money should be centralized as far as possible. An exception may be the circulation desk, for it would be counterproductive to attempt to direct users elsewhere. In large libraries or those with branches there may be several such desks. In any case, care must always be taken to provide the appropriate equipment for the handling and storage of money.

It is essential to keep full records, particularly where there are massive invoices from vendors or other suppliers that have to be matched against internal costs and charges. While it may not seem necessary to keep records of such simple charges as overdues, documentation is a protection against lawsuits and provides an adequate record of the level of compliance. The use of a cash register may be appropriate, or it may be necessary to program the automated circulation system to provide records. Where the lending records are maintained by a regional system, it may be difficult to work in the local library's records of payment, though there will be a clear record of overdues. Other transactions may require more elaborate recordkeeping, for instance online searches or personal Internet use. Computer programs are available for this kind of recordkeeping, and the library should consider using them. Most vendors will provide detailed accounts of system use, and the library can work from these, but the time is near when much activity will be conducted in cyberspace. Libraries must, consequently, be prepared to construct their own local records.

Differentiation between classes of user is much more complex, and the resulting decisions will depend on the goals of the institution. Internal and external users present fewer problems than different local users, who may have special needs or require special treatment. External students may also require special consideration. Fees and charges should be constructed with these variations in mind. There may also be legal considerations. While public libraries are often governed by state legislation, other kinds of libraries may have different kinds of controls.[8] Beyond this lie even more complex considerations based on contract law that may enable suppliers to limit access to their products. All these issues must be considered when libraries are contemplating charging for their services.

NOTES

1. David W. Penniman, "On Their Terms: Preparing Libraries for a Competitive Environment," *Bottom Line* 1, no. 3 (1987): 11–15; also Alice Size Warner, *Making Money: Fees for Library Services* (New York: Neal-Schuman Publishers, Inc., 1989), and "Charging Back, Charging Out, Charging Fees," *Bottom Line* 4, no. 3 (1990): 32–35.

2. Philip M. Ray, "Information Economics and Libraries in the Digital Age," *Bottom Line* 9, no. 2 (1996): 29–34.

3. Michael E. Koenig and Johanna Goforth, "Libraries and the Cost Recovery Imperative: The Emergence of the Issue," *IFAL Journal* 19 (1993): 261–279; also Mary Jo Lynch, *Financing Online Search Services in Publicly Supported Libraries* (Chicago: American Library Association, 1982).

4. Murray S. Martin, *Collection Development and Finance: A Guide to Strategic Library-Materials Budgeting* (Chicago: American Library Association, 1995). A sequel on resource budgeting is in process. Resource budgeting, however, requires a complete rethinking of the ways in which the library constructs and uses its budget. Even program budgets have usually failed to look carefully at the ways in which library materials expenditures should be allocated and the alternatives presented by different programs in terms of their ability to serve the user.

5. Diane Tebbetts, "What Library Services Really Cost," *Bottom Line* 6, no. 1 (1992): 19–23; also Darlene E. Weingand, "What Do Products/Services Cost? How Do We Know?" *Library Trends* 43 (Winter 1995): 401–408.

6. Coopers & Lybrand, *Valuing the Economic Costs and Benefits of Libraries* (Wellington: New Zealand Library and Information Association, 1996). Some of the same concerns are shown in Nancy Van House's *Public Library User Fees: The Use and Financing of Public Libraries* (Westport, Conn.: Greenwood Press, 1983).

7. Alice Duhon Mancini, "Evaluating Commercial Document Suppliers: Improving Access to Current Journal Literature," *College & Research Libraries* 57, no. 2 (March 1996): 123–131.

8. Pete Giacomo, *The Fee or Free Decision: Legal, Economic, Political, and Ethical Perspectives for Public Libraries* (New York: Neal-Schuman Publishers, Inc., 1989); and Wendy D. Wood, "A Librarian's Guide to Fee-Based Services," *The Reference Librarian* 40 (1993): 121–129. The latter looks at some of the legal implications of charging for services in academic libraries.

Bibliography

Ardis, Susan B., and Karen S. Croneis. "Document Delivery, Cost Containment and Serial Ownership." *College & Research Library News* 48 (November 1987): 624–627.

Arms, Caroline, ed. *Campus Strategies for Libraries and Electronic Information*. Bedford, Mass.: Digital Press, 1990.

Association for Library Collections and Technical Services. Reproduction of Library Materials Section. Photocopy Costs in Libraries Committee. "Report of the Photocopy Costs in Libraries Committee." *Library Resources & Technical Services* 14, no. 2 (1970): 279–289.

Association of College and Research Libraries. Standards and Accreditation Committee. "Guidelines for Extended-campus Library Services." *College & Research Libraries News* 50, no. 5 (1989): 404–406.

Baker, Sharon L., and F. Wilford Lancaster. *The Measurement and Evaluation of Library Services*. 2nd ed. Arlington, Va.: Information Resources Press, 1991.

Baumol, William J., and Mattityahu Marcus. *The Economics of Academic Libraries*. Washington D. C.: American Council on Education, 1973.

———, and Sue Ann Batey Blackman. "Electronics, the Cost Disease, and the Operation of Libraries." *Journal of the American Society of Information Science* 34 (1983): 181–191.

Berman, Barbara L. "Videos in Public Libraries: Free or Fee?" *Public and School Libraries* (1994): 29–35.

Bierman, Kenneth J. "How Will Libraries Pay for Electronic Information?" *Journal of Library Administration* 15, no. 3/4 (1991): 67–84.

Blake, Fay M. "What's a Nice Librarian Like You Doing Behind a Cash Register?" In *User Fees: A Practical Perspective*, edited by Miriam A. Drake, 43–49. Littleton, Colo.: Libraries Unlimited, 1981.

Boucher, Virgina. *Interlibrary Loan Practices Handbook*. 2nd ed. Chicago: American Library Association, 1996.

Bremer, Suzanne W. *Long Range Planning: A How-To-Do-It Manual for Public Libraries*. New York: Neal-Schuman Publishers, Inc., 1994.

Broncolini, Kristine, and Rich E. Provine. *Video Collections and Multimedia in ARL Libraries*. (Spec Kit no. 199). Washington, D.C.: Association of Research Libraries, Office of Management Services, 1993.

Burgin, Robert, and Patsy Hansel. "Library Overdues: An Update." *Library and Archival Security* 10, no. 2 (1990): 51– 75.

Butos, Roxann, comp. *Interlibrary Loan in College Libraries*. (CLIP Note #6). Chicago: ACRL, 1993.

Carpenter, Michael. "How Can We Improve Resource Sharing? A Scholar's View." *Advances in Library Resource Sharing* 1 (1990): 59–73.

Christianson, Elin B., David E. King, and Janet L. Ahronsfeld. *Special Libraries: A Guide for Management*. 3rd ed. Washington, D.C.: Special Libraries Association, 1991.

Chrzastowski, Tina E., and Karen A. Schmidt. "Surveying the Damage: Academic Library Serial Cancellations 1987–88 through 1989–90." *College & Research Libraries* 54, no. 2 (March 1993): 93–102.

Citron, Helen R., and James B. Dodd. "Cost Allocation and Cost Recovery Considerations in a Special Academic Library." *Science and Technology Libraries* 5 (Winter 1984): 1–14.

Commings, Karen. "Libraries in the Future—Carroll County Public Library Offers Internet Access." *Computers in Libraries* 14 (April 1995): 14–15.

Conference on Fee-Based Research in College and University Libraries. Proceedings of the Meetings at the C. W. Post Center of

Long Island University, Greenvale, N. Y., June 17–18, 1982. 1983.

Coopers & Lybrand. *Valuing the Economic Costs and Benefits of Libraries.* Wellington: New Zealand Library and Information Association, 1996.

Cortez, Ed, and Robin Rice. "An Investigation into the Role of Public Libraries with Online Reference Service." *Public Library Quarterly* 14, no. 2/3 (1994): 7–27.

Costa, Betty, and Marie Costa, with Larry Costa. *A Micro Handbook for Small Libraries and Media Centers.* 3rd ed. Englewood, Colo.: Libraries Unlimited, 1991.

Crawford, Gregory A. "Research Notes: A Conjoint Analysis of Reference Services in Academic Libraries." *College & Research Libraries* 55 (May 1994): 257–267.

Curzon, Susan Carol. *Managing Change: The How-To-Do-It Manual for Planning, Implementing, and Evaluating Change in Libraries.* New York: Neal-Schuman Publishers, Inc., 1993.

Dorr, Raize. "Planning Photocopy Services: A Success Story." *Bottom Line* 5, no. 1 (1989): 21–26.

Drake, Miriam A., ed. *User Fees: A Practical Perspective.* Littleton, Colo.: Libraries Unlimited, 1981.

DuBrin, Andrew J. *Contemporary Applied Management: The How-To-Do-It Manual for Planning, Implementing, and Evaluating Change in Libraries.* New York: Neal-Schuman Publishers, Inc., 1989.

Dunn, John A. Jr., and Murray S. Martin. "The Whole Cost of Libraries," *Library Trends* 42 (Winter 1994): 564–578.

Dutchak, Arlene M. "A Look at What's Happening in Alberta: User Fees: Hidden Taxes or Free Enterprise?" *Pacific Northwest Library Association Quarterly* 58 (Spring 1994): 11–12.

Ellsworth Associates. *Study of Cities and County Library Services. Final Report.* Palo Alto, Calif.: Ellsworth Associates, 1991.

Erickson, Rodney. "*Choice* for Collection Development." *Library Acquisitions: Practice and Theory* 16, no. 1 (1992): 43–49.

Ernest, D. J. "Academic Libraries, Fee-based Information Services, and the Business Community." *RQ* 32 (Spring 1993): 393–402.

"Fees for Library Service: Current Practice and Future Policy." *Collection Building* 8, no. 1 (1987). Special issue.

Finet, Scott. "Options in Offering a Photocopy Service." *Bottom Line* 5, no. 3 (Fall 1991): 18–24.

Fortune, Joan. "Budgeting." In *Online Searching: The Basics, Settings & Management*, edited by Joann H. Lee. Littleton, Colo.: Libraries Unlimited, 1984.

Gell, Marilyn Killebrew. "User Fees I: The Economic Argument." *Library Journal* (January 1, 1979): 19–23.

————. "User Fees II: The Library Response." *Library Journal* (15 January 1979): 170–173.

Getz, Malcolm. "Document Delivery." *Bottom Line* 5, no. 4 (Winter 1991–92): 40–44.

————. "Increasing the Value of User Time." *Bottom Line* 1, no. 2 (1987): 37–39.

————. "Pricing Photocopies." *Bottom Line* 1, no. 1 (1987): 43–45.

————. *Public Libraries: An Economic View*. Baltimore, Md.: Johns Hopkins University Press, 1980.

Giacoma, Pete. *The Fee or Free Decision: Legal, Economic, Political, and Ethical Perspectives for Public Libraries*. New York: Neal-Schuman Publishers, Inc., 1989.

————. "User Fees: Pros and Cons." *Bottom Line* 3, no. 1 (1989): 27–30.

Grotenhuis, Albert J. te, and Selma J. Heijnekamp. "The User Pays: Cost Billing in a Company Library." *Bottom Line* 8, no. 4 (1995): 26–31. First published in *Library Management* 15, no. 4 (1994.)

Hayes, Sherman. "Budgeting for and Controlling the Cost of *Other* in Library Expenditure: The Distant Relative in the Budgeting Process." In *Financial Planning for Libraries*, edited by Murray S. Martin, 121–131. New York: Haworth Press, 1983.

Haynes, Craig, comp. *Providing Public Services to Remote Users*. SPEC Kit 191. Washington, D. C.: Association of Research Libraries, Systems and Procedures Exchange Center, 1993.

Herman, Larry. "Costing, Charging, and Pricing: Related But Different Decisions." *Bottom Line* 4, no. 2 (Summer 1990): 26–28.

Higginbotham, Barbra Buckner, and Sally Bowdoin. *Access Versus Assets: A Comprehensive Guide to Resource Sharing for Academic Libraries*. Chicago: American Library Association, 1993.

Holt, Glen E., Donald Elliott, and Christopher Dussold. "A Framework for Evaluating Public Investment in Urban Libraries." *Bottom Line* 9, no. 4 (1996): 4–13.

Hubbard, William J., and J. Patrick O'Brien. "Price Elasticity of Library Photocopies: An Empirical Demonstration of the Law of Demand." *Collection Management* 19, no. 1/2 (1994): 101–109.

Intellectual Property and the National Information Infrastructure: The Report of the Working Group on Intellectual Property Rights. Chair, Bruce A. Lehman. Washington, D.C.: Department of Commerce, 1995.

Jackson, Mary E. "Library to Library: To Charge or Not to Charge?" *Wilson Library Bulletin* 67 (June 1993): 94–95+.

Jarvelin, Kalervo. "A Methodology for User Charge Estimation in Numeric Online Databanks, Part I: A Review of Numeric Databanks and Charging Principles." *Journal of Information Science* 14 (1988): 3–16.

————. "A Methodology for User Charge Estimation in Numeric Online Databanks, Part II." *Journal of Information Science* 14 (1988): 77–92.

————. "A Straightforward Method for Advance Estimation of User Charges for Information in Numeric Databases." *Journal of Documentation* 42 (June 1986): 65–83.

Kahkonen, Laura. "What Is Your Library Worth?" *Bottom Line* 5, no. 1 (1991): 9.

Kascus, Marie, and William Aguilar. "Providing Library Support to Off-Campus Programs." *College & Research Libraries* 49, no. 1 (January, 1988): 29–37.

Katz, William A. *Introduction to Reference Work.* 2 vols. 6th ed. New York: McGraw-Hill, 1992.

Kehoe, Brendon P. *Zen and the Art of the Internet: A Beginner's Guide.* Englewood Cliffs, N.J.: Prentice-Hall, 1994.

Kendrick, Aubrey W. "Computer Database Searching and Business Libraries," *Online Review* 12 (February 1988): 39–46.

Kennedy, Sue. "The Role of Commercial Document Delivery Services in Interlibrary Loan." In *Research Access through New Technology,* edited by Mary E. Jackson, 68–81. New York: AMS Press, 1989.

Ketterer, B. A. "Library Automation Consortia: What Fees Should Members Pay?" *Bottom Line* 6, no. 2 (Summer/Fall 1992): 23–27.

Knight, Douglas M., and E. Shepley Nourse, ed. *Libraries at Large: Tradition, Innovation and the Public Interest.* N.Y.: Bowker, 1969.

Koenig, Michael E., and Johanna Goforth. "Libraries and the Cost Recovery Imperative: The Emergence of the Issue." *IFAL Journal* 19 (1993): 261–279.

Krol, E. V. *The Whole Internet: User's Guide & Catalog.* 2nd ed. Sebastopol, Calif.: O'Reilly and Associates.

Kurosman, Kathleen, and Barbara Ammerman Durniak. "Document Delivery: A Comparison of Commercial Document Suppliers and Interlibrary Loan Services." *College & Research Libraries* 55, no. 2 (March 1994): 129–139.

Laber, Karen Nadder. "The Internet and the Public Library: Practical and Political Realities." *Internet Librarian* 13 (October 1993): 65–70.

Ladley, Barbara. "Questions to Ask." *Bottom Line* 2, no. 2 (1988): 17.

Lee, Joann H., ed. *Online Searching: The Basics, Settings & Management.* Littleton, Colo.: Libraries Unlimited, 1984.

Lynch, Clifford. "Pricing Electronic Reference Works: The Dilemma of the Mixed Library and Consumer Marketplace." In *Issues in Collection Management: Librarians, Booksellers, Publishers,* edited by Murray S. Martin, 19–34. Greenwich, Conn.: JAI Press, 1995.

Lynch, Mary Jo. *Financing Online Search Services in Publicly Supported Libraries: The Report of an ALA Survey.* Chicago: American Library Association, 1982.

————. "How Wired Are We? New Data on Library Technology." *College & Research Library News* 57, no. 2 (February 1996): 97–100.

McCabe, Gerard B., ed. *The Smaller Academic Library: A Management Handbook.* Westport, Conn.: Greenwood, 1988.

McCarthy, Kevin, and others. "Exploring Benefit-Based Finance for Local Government Services: Must User Charges Harm the Disadvantaged?" In *Charging for Computer-Based Reference*

Services, edited by Peter G. Watson, 3–16. Chicago: Reference and Adult Services Division, American Library Association, 1978.

McClure, Charles R., John C. Bertot, and John C. Beachboard. *Internet Costs and Cost Models for Public Libraries: Final Report*. Washington, D. C.: U. S. National Commission on Libraries and Information Science, June 1995.

————, ————, and Douglas L. Zweizig. *Public Libraries and the Internet: Study Results, Policy Issues, and Recommendations*. Washington, D. C.: National Commission on Libraries and Information Science, June 1994.

Mancini, Alice Duhon. "Evaluating Commercial Document Suppliers: Improving Access to Current Journal Literature." *College & Research Libraries* 57, no. 2 (March 1996): 123–131.

Martin, Murray S. *Collection Development and Finance: A Guide to Strategic Library-Materials Budgeting*. Chicago: American Library Association, 1995.

————. "Economic Barriers to Information Access." *Bottom Line* 7, no. 1 (Summer 1993): 3–4.

————. "The Implications for Acquisitions of Stagnant Budgets." *The Acquisitions Librarian* 2 (1989): 105–117.

————. "Money Matters: The Cost of the Internet." *Technicalities* 15 (March 1995): 1, 5.

————. "Stagnant Budgets and Their Effects on Academic Libraries." *Bottom Line* 3, no. 3 (1989): 10–16.

Massis, Bruce E., and Winnie Vitzansky, comp. "Interlibrary Loan of Alternative Format Materials: A Balanced Source Book." *Journal of Interlibrary Loan & Information Supply* 3, no. 1/2 (1992). Special issue.

Mielke, Linda, "Short-range Planning for Turbulent Times, " *American Libraries* 26, no. 9 (October 1995): 905–906.

Miller, Connie, and Patricia Tagler. "An Analysis of Interlibrary Loan and Commercial Document Supply Performance." *Library Quarterly* 58 (October 1988): 352–366.

Morris, Leslie R. *Interlibrary Loan Policies Directory*. 5th ed. New York: Neal-Schuman Publishers, Inc., 1995.

Mosely, M. M. "What Should Be "Free" at the Library? [Florida statutes need clarification]" *Florida Libraries* 36 (November 1993): 171–172.

Mount, Ellis. *Special Libraries and Information Centers: An Introductory Text.* 2nd ed. Washington, D. C.: Special Libraries Association, 1991.

Mushkin, Selma J., and Richard M. Bird. "Public Prices: An Overview." In *Public Prices for Public Products*, edited by Selma J. Mushkin, 3–25. Washington, D.C.: Urban Institute, 1972.

National Commission on Libraries and Information Science. "The Role of Fees in Supporting Library and Information Services in Public and Academic Libraries." *Collection Building* 8, no. 1 (1987): 3–17.

Nazri, William Z. "Reprography." In *Encyclopedia of Library and Information Science*, edited by Allen Kent, Harold Lancour, and Jay E. Daly, vol. 25, 236–279. New York: Marcel Dekker, 1978.

Nista, Ann S., Karen M. Albert, and Beth M. Lewis. "Cost Recovery and Usage Tracking of CD-ROM Databases with Menuing Software." *Medical Reference Quarterly* 10, no. 4 (Winter 1991): 15–27.

Pease, Barbara, and Colleen Power. "Reference Services for Off-Campus Students and Faculty." In *Reference Services Planning in the 90s*, edited by Gail Z. Eckwright and Lori McKeenan, 43–62. New York: Haworth, 1989.

Pederson, Wayne, and David Gregory. "Interlibrary Loan and Commercial Document Supply: Finding the Right Fit." *Journal of Academic Librarianship* 20, no. 5/6 (November 1994): 263–272.

Penniman, W. David. "On Their Terms: Preparing Libraries for a Competitive Environment." *Bottom Line* 1, no. 3 (1987): 11–15.

Photocopy Services in ARL Libraries. SPEC Kit no. 115. Washington, D. C.: Association of Research Libraries, Systems and Procedures Exchange Center, 1985.

Public Library Association. Public Policy for Public Libraries Section. Fee-Based Services Committee. *Position Paper on Fee-Based Services.* 1996.

Quint, Barbara. "Connect Time: Where's Your Parachute?" *Wilson Library Bulletin* 66 (April 1992): 86–86.

Ray, Philip M. "Information Economics and Libraries in the Digital Age." *Bottom Line* 9, no. 2 (1996): 29–34.

Richmond, Charles W. "Free or Fee Based Library Service in the Year 2000," *Journal of Library Administration* 11 (1989): 111–118.

Richmond, Elizabeth. "Cost Finding: Method and Management." *Bottom Line* 1, no. 4 (1987): 16–20.

Roche, Marilyn M. *ARL/RLG Interlibrary Loan Cost Study*. Washington, D. C.: Association of Research Libraries, 1993.

Rogers, Rutherford D., and David C. Weber. *University Library Administration*. New York: H.W. Wilson, 1971.

Saffady, William. *Introduction to Automation for Libraries*. 3rd ed. Chicago: American Library Association, 1994.

Sallis, Philip. "The Semantics of Cost Recovery or User Pays." *New Zealand Libraries* 14, no. 4 (1991): 5–7.

Sawyer, Rod. "The Economic and Job Creation Benefits of Ontario Public Libraries." *Bottom Line* 9, no. 4 (1996): 14–26.

Smith, Wendy. "Fee-based Services: Are They Worth It?" *Library Journal* 118 (15 June 1993): 40–43.

Snyder, Carolyne A., and James Fox, ed. *Libraries and Distance Learning*. Greenwich, Conn.: JAI Press, 1997.

Stein, Barbara L., and Risa W. Brown. *Running a School Library Media Center: A How-To-Do-It Manual for Libraries*. New York: Neal-Schuman Publishers, Inc., 1992.

Steuart, Robert D., and Barbara B. Moran. *Library and Information Center Management*. 4th ed. Englewood, Colo.: Libraries Unlimited, 1993.

Talaga, James A. "Concept of Price in a Library Context." *Journal of Library Administration* 14, no. 4 (1991): 87–101.

Taylor, David C. "Serials Management: Issues and Recommendations." In *Issues in Library Management: A Reader for the Professional Librarian*, 82–96. White Plains, N. Y.: Knowledge Industry Publications, 1984.

Taylor, Suzanne and C. Brigid Welsh, ed. *Provision of Computer Printing Capabilities to Library Patrons*. SPEC Kit 183. Washington, D. C.: Association of Research Libraries, 1992.

Tebbetts, Diane, "What Library Services Really Cost," *Bottom Line* 6, no. 1 (1992): 19–23.

Tilson, Yvette. "Income Generation and Pricing in Libraries." *Bottom Line* 8, no. 2 (1995): 23–26.

Trail, Mary Ann. "Fee-Based Services: Do They Have a Place in Our Libraries?" *New Jersey Libraries* 27 (Winter 1993–94): 22–24.

Truesdell, Cheryl B. "Is Access a Viable Alternative to Ownership? A Review of Access Performance." *Journal of Academic Librarianship* 20, no. 4 (September 1994): 200–206.

"ULC Reports Most Members without Fee-charging Policies; An Urban Libraries Council Survey Finds that More than Half of Its Members Charge for Online Databases and That Most of Them Have Fees Policies in Disarray." *Library Journal* 118 (1 May 1993): 14–15.

Van House, Nancy. *Public Library User Fees: The Use and Financing of Public Libraries*. Westport, Conn.: Greenwood Press, 1983.

Waldhart, Thomas J. "Patterns of Interlibrary Loan in the United States: A Review of Research." *Library and Information Science Research* 7 (1988): 209–229.

————. "Performance Evaluation of Interlibrary Loan in the United States: A Review of Research." *Library and Information Science Research* 7 (1988): 313–331.

Wallace, Linda K. "Advocating Equity: ALA's New Campaign." *College & Research Libraries News* 57, no. 2 (February 1996): 78.

Warner, Alice Size. "Charging Back, Charging Out, Charging Fees." *Bottom Line* 4, no. 3 (1990): 32–35.

————. *Making Money: Fees for Library Services*. New York: Neal-Schuman Publishers, Inc., 1989.

Weaver, Sherill, and Harold A. Shaffer. "Contracting to Provide Library Service for a Distance Graduate Education Program." *Bottom Line* 8, no. 3 (1995): 20–27.

Weingand, Darlene E. *Administration of the Small Public Library*. 3rd ed. Chicago: American Library Association, 1992.

————. "What Do Products/Services Cost? How Do We Know?" *Library Trends* 43 (Winter 1995): 401–408.

White, Herbert. "The Value-Added Process of Librarianship." *Library Journal* 114, no. 1 (January 1989): 62–63.

Whitson, William L. "The Way I See It: Fee, Free, or Subsidy? The Future Role of Libraries." *College & Research Library News* 55, no. 7 (July-August 1994): 426–427.

Williams, Thomas L., Henry L. Lemkau, and Suzetta Burrows. "The Economics of Academic Health Sciences Libraries: Cost Recovery in the Era of Big Science." *Bulletin of the Medical Library Association* 76 (October 1988): 317–322.

Wood, Frances K. "When Do Dollars for Information Make Sense? The Wisconsin ISD Experience." *Bottom Line* 1, no. 4 (1987): 25–27.

Wood, Wendy D. "A Librarian's Guide to Fee-Based Services" [legal barriers in academic libraries] *The Reference Librarian* 40 (1993): 121–129.

Young, Peter R. "Changing Information Access Economics: New Roles for Libraries and Librarians." *Information Technology and Libraries* 13, no. 2 (June 1994): 103–114.

Index

About the Authors

Murray Martin was born and educated in New Zealand, with degrees in English, Accounting, and Library Science. He has worked in academic and special libraries in New Zealand, Canada, and the United States, both in acquisitions and administration, and has taught several courses in English and Comparative Literature. He retired from Tufts University after nine years as University Librarian and Professor of Library Science Emeritus, and continues to write, consult, and speak on library topics. He has a special interest in library finance and collection management. Over the years he has written several books—*Budgetary Control in Academic Libraries* (JAI Press, 1978), *Issues in Personnel Management in Academic Libraries* (JAI Press, 1981), *Academic Library Budgets* (JAI Press, 1993), *Collection Management and Finance: A Guide to Strategic Library Materials Budgeting* (ALA Editions, 1995), and *Resource Budgeting* (ALA Editions, 1997)—and numerous articles. He has been active in several library associations. He currently contributes financial columns to *Technicalities* and *The Bottom Line: Managing Library Finances*. In retirement, he has had more time to devote to his other lifetime interest, Commonwealth Literature, and has also given papers and written articles in this field.

Betsy Park is Head of the Reference Department at the University of Memphis Libraries. She holds a B.A. from Stanford University, an M.L.S. from the State University of New York in Buffalo, and an M.S. (in Education) from Memphis State University. She has held a wide range of positions in academic libraries from 1980 to the present. She has written extensively for a variety of professional journals including *College and Research Libraries, Journal of Academic Librarianship*, and *The Bottom Line: Managing Library Finances*. She is very active in the Association of College and Research Libraries and currently serves as Chair of its Instruction Section's 1998 Conference Planning Committee.